Let There Be Light

Let There Be Light

❖

A Book About Windows

ILLUSTRATED WITH PHOTOGRAPHS AND PRINTS

JAMES CROSS GIBLIN

THOMAS Y. CROWELL   NEW YORK

Let There Be Light: A Book About Windows
Copyright © 1988 by James Cross Giblin

Library of Congress Cataloging-in-Publication Data

Giblin, James.
    Let there be light : a book about windows / James Cross Giblin.
      — 1st ed.
      p.   cm.
    Bibliography: p.
    Includes index.
    Summary: Surveys the development of windows
from prehistory to the modern era.
    ISBN 0-690-04693-6 : $
    ISBN 0-690-04695-2 (lib. bdg.) : $
    1. Windows—Juvenile literature. [1. Windows.] I. Title.
TH2275.G53 1988   87-35052
690'.1823'09—dc 19   CIP
                                         AC

Typography by Christine Kettner
2 3 4 5 6 7 8 9 10

COURTESY OF THE METROPOLITAN MUSEUM OF ART, FLETCHER FUND, 1919.

Frontispiece :
St. Jerome in his study. Engraving by Albrecht Dürer (1471−1528).

ACKNOWLEDGMENTS

❖

For their help in providing inspiration, research material, and illustrations, the author thanks the following individuals, institutions, and corporations: Carole S. Adler; Sue Alexander; The American Museum of Natural History; The British Museum; The British Tourist Authority; John Burgee Architects; The Cleveland Museum of Art; Foundation for San Francisco's Architectural Heritage; Russell Freedman; French Government Tourist Office; Anna Cross Giblin; Morrell Gipson; Hedrich-Blessing Photographers; Dianne Hess; Japan National Tourist Organization; The Jewish Theological Seminary of America; Lever Brothers Company; The Library of Congress, Prints and Photographs Division; Murray Liebman; Davida N. List; The Metropolitan Museum of Art; The Museum of Modern Art, New York; The National Gallery of Art, Washington; National Museum of American Art, Smithsonian Institution; The Netherlands Board of Tourism; The New York Public Library; The Oakland Museum, California; PPG Industries, Inc.; Jeanne Prahl; Beatrice Schenk de Regniers; Rolscreen Company and Burson-Marsteller; UPI/Bettmann Newsphotos.

FOR BARBARA FENTON

"I know of nothing so beneficent as windows. Fie upon the ungrateful man who has no window-god in his house, and thinks himself too great a philosopher to bow down to windows! May he live in a place without windows for a while to teach him the value of windows. As for me I will keep up the high worship of windows till I come to the windowless grave."

—Hilaire Belloc,
in *The Path to Rome*

CONTENTS

❖

Let There Be Light

FROM MY WINDOWS

❖

I live on the fourteenth floor of a high-rise apartment house in New York City, and the windows in my living room face south. On clear days I can see the 107-story twin towers of the World Trade Center glittering in the sun. On stormy nights I've watched sheets of rain pour down and jumped when I've seen jagged bolts of lightning strike the Center's towers.

As I've looked out my windows, I've marveled at how strong they are. The thin glass panes keep out the extremes of heat and cold, as well as rain and snow, while at the same time allowing me to see vast distances. But I know they're also extremely vulnerable. A well-aimed rock could shatter one of them in an instant, as many rocks and other missiles thrown by angry people have shattered windows throughout history.

This book was inspired by the view from my windows and my musing about them. As I pursued the idea, I found

1

myself becoming increasingly fascinated. I'd never imagined that windows had played a role in so many dramatic events, or that they revealed so much about the lives of people in every part of the world. My hope is that you, the reader, will share my fascination, and that after finishing this book you will look at—and through—your own windows in new and different ways.

—J.C.G.

ONE

❖

To See the World Outside

When you wake up in the morning, your room is probably dark and shadowy. You climb out of bed and pick your way across the rug, being careful not to stumble over anything. Reaching the window, you fling back the drapes or raise the blind. Light floods the room, and you look out to see what kind of day it's going to be.

Our modern world is full of windows. Clear glass windows admit light and air into our homes and schools, and into the factories and office buildings where people work. Our eyes are caught by striking displays in the windows of mall shops and downtown department stores. Stained-glass windows fill our houses of worship with brilliant patterns of color and light.

Most of us take all these windows for granted. If we think about it at all, we probably assume that people always had them. But that isn't so. There was a time when glass windows were a luxury only the rich could afford. Before that, windows of any kind were a rarity. And before that, when our ancestors lived in caves, their only "window" was likely to be the opening at the entrance.

When people of the Stone Age began to construct their own shelters about 12,000 years ago, those shelters didn't have windows either. Like the American Indian tipi, such a shelter was probably circular in shape and was built by leaning together a group of branches to form a cone. The builders tied the branches together at the top with vines and covered the framework with animal skins or a thatch made of reeds. The only openings in the dwelling would be a low entranceway and perhaps a hole at the top to allow smoke from the central hearth to escape.

Although they were neither very sturdy nor very comfortable, shelters of this type served the basic needs of people who moved about a great deal in search of wild animals and plants for food. Like tipis and tents, they could be put up quickly in a new place and taken down just as quickly when the tribe had exhausted the local food supplies and needed to travel on.

This nomadic way of life continued for centuries. Then, about nine or ten thousand years ago, it began to change for many people throughout the world. Starting in the Middle East, men and women learned how to domesticate wild cattle, horses, sheep, and goats, and how to raise crops of wheat, oats, and barley instead of gathering wild grasses

Blackfoot Indian tipi. Photo by Thane L. Bierwert.

and nuts. No longer did people have to move about constantly in search of food. Now they could farm in one spot and enjoy the comforts of permanent dwellings.

Few of these dwellings had windows, however. Most of them were circular in shape, like the temporary shelters they replaced. In northern Europe they were usually built of stones which were piled in more or less regular rows that gradually came closer together until they formed cones.

Sometimes, as in tipi-type structures, an opening was left at the top of a round hut so smoke could escape. There would be an entrance, too, but it was usually small and low in order to prevent loss of heat from the central fire. Otherwise the hut was windowless and dark. In fact, in the Scottish islands where some people still live in such dwellings, they are known as "black houses."

Windowless circular houses were also built in Africa, but there they were made of wooden poles and plaster instead of stones. The poles were cut when they were green and

Ruins of prehistoric circular stone dwellings at Jarlshof in the Shetland Isles, Scotland.
COURTESY OF THE BRITISH TOURIST AUTHORITY.

Circular dwellings of woven reeds and thatch in a central African village. Note mat covering doorway in hut at the center.

flexible, so that they could be tied together with various natural fibers at the top. The walls were usually filled in with brushwood and mud, plastered over with a mixture of cow dung and ashes.

Light entered these African houses through a doorway, and often there were two openings—one at the front and another at the side or back—to allow for cross-ventilation. Instead of having doors, the openings were covered with screens made of woven reeds. The owners put the screens in place at night before they went to sleep and before they went away during the day. But whenever they were home, they set the screens aside so that sunshine and fresh air could come into their dwellings.

The first people to install actual windows in their houses may have been the Eskimos who lived in what is today Alaska, Canada, and Greenland. Light was, and is, a precious thing in those far-northern regions where days are short and winter lasts for almost ten months of the year. And unlike people in warm climates, the Eskimos could not rely on open entrances to provide light.

To solve this problem, the Eskimos devised several unusual kinds of windows. Those who lived in Canada spent the winter in circular dwellings made of firmly packed blocks of snow. Midway up the dome-shaped houses, they substituted one or more blocks of clear, freshwater ice for the usual snow blocks. The ice blocks were translucent, which means that light could come through them. So they made effective windows even though a person couldn't really see in or out of them.

The Alaskan and Greenland Eskimos lived in winter houses of logs or stones, piled high with layers of sod to keep out the cold. Fresh air blew into this kind of house through the entrance tunnel and was warmed by the heat from blubber lamps. Stale air and smoke escaped through a tiny hole in the roof. The only natural light in the dwelling came through a window of translucent gut taken from the stomach of a seal or walrus. The window was usually set into the house above the entrance passage. Instead of being stretched across a wooden frame, the pane of gut was sewn into a square opening cut in a seal hide that formed part of the wall.

At an early date, in those parts of the world that had abundant trees and forests, many people stopped building

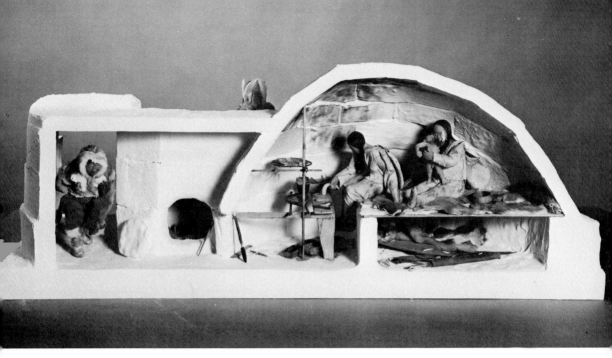

Cutaway model of Eskimo igloo. A window of clear ice is directly above the cookpot. Photo by Rota.

Cutaway view of Eskimo winter house. The edge of the translucent gut window is visible above the entrance tunnel. Photo by Rota.

circular dwellings and started constructing rectangular wooden houses. Archaeologists have found the remains of such houses along the banks of the Danube River and the shores of Swiss lakes. Some of them go back as far as 7000 B.C.

Timber construction led naturally to a rectangular shape, since tree trunks are generally straight. When they are laid horizontally at the base of a wall to form the foundation or to edge the floor, they produce a house with straight sides.

The most common wooden structure was the framed type, in which posts were set vertically in the ground at a distance from one another, and the tops were joined by horizontal timbers. The wall areas between the posts were filled in with screens that were designed to shut out the weather and protect the inhabitants, but not to support the main structure. In northern Europe these screens usually consisted of intertwined twigs and branches, coated heavily on both sides with mud plaster.

As people learned to make better building materials, mud plaster gave way to stuccos of lime and cement, and even in some places to brick. The construction principle remained the same, however: The posts did the supporting, while the walls, whatever their material, served merely as protecting screens. And it was easy to cut into them to make windows.

Like the Eskimos, people living in the colder, darker regions of Scandinavia and Russia had the most need of windows in their rectangular wooden dwellings. The openings were usually small and narrow to keep out the cold weather that prevailed for most of the year. Since no one had yet discovered how to make glass, people covered these window openings with layers of a translucent material such as mica or with thin, translucent fish bladders.

Even though the ancient lands of the Middle East lacked large supplies of timber, people living there soon adopted the rectangular form of construction for their mud-brick and stone buildings. The foundations of rectangular dwellings dating to between 6000 and 7000 B.C. have been found at Jericho in Israel and at Catal Huyuk in Turkey.

People in the Middle East, like people elsewhere, turned to rectangular construction because it offered more usable space within the dwelling. Beds, benches, and other items of furniture could be fitted more easily into rooms with corners than into round or oval ones. Rectangular units could also be joined together to form a house of many rooms, or a line of buildings along a village street.

By 6000 B.C., at Jericho and Catal Huyuk and other sites in the Middle East, people were beginning to cluster together in towns of several thousand inhabitants or more. Soon the world's first cities would arise in Mesopotamia, that ancient seat of civilization located between the Tigris and Euphrates rivers. In these crowded cities light and air became more precious than ever, and people had to find new ways to obtain them through the windows in their homes and temples.

TWO

❖

Windows for People and Gods

The ancient town of Catal Huyuk had no streets, and no windows in the exterior walls of its dwellings. The huge block of windowless buildings presented a continuous blank wall to any enemy that might threaten the town.

Two or three thousand people probably lived in Catal Huyuk, which covered more than thirty-two acres and was inhabited from about 6500 to about 5500 B.C. When archaeologists unearthed the town's ruins in the 1960s, they discovered that its rectangular mud-brick houses, consisting of several rooms, were connected to each other by small yards. The only way in or out of a house was through an opening in the flat roof, and in many of the houses that was also the main entrance for light and air.

A similar type of architecture developed much later in the American southwest—and again for defensive reasons. There, between A.D. 1100 and 1300, the Pueblo Indians built towns of several hundred people on high mesas or in narrow river gorges.

Like the dwellings in Catal Huyuk, the one-room Pueblo houses of clay and stone were set next to one another, forming a single continuous building. In the middle there was often an open square. The one-story, flat-roofed houses had no doors or windows, only hatches in the roofs. People entered a house by climbing a ladder from the ground to the roof, and then climbing down another ladder into the room below. The open hatch also allowed light and air to enter the house, and smoke from the cook fire to escape.

The ladders could be pulled up quickly onto the roofs if an enemy attacked the pueblo. In case of rain or a sudden dust storm, a thin sheet of sandstone was drawn over each hatch to protect the inhabitants of the house. Sometimes this cover was propped up with a rock at one end so that rain would run down it while a little light and air still got into the room below.

As the population of the Pueblo village grew, and the hilltop or gorge filled with more and more houses, the only place to build additional dwellings was upward. Accordingly,

Top: *Ruins of the pueblo at Walpi in Arizona. Photo by R. E. Logan.*
COURTESY OF THE AMERICAN MUSEUM OF NATURAL HISTORY.

Bottom: *Model showing daily activities of the Pueblo Indians inside their multistory dwellings. Photo by Thane L. Bierwert.*
COURTESY OF THE AMERICAN MUSEUM OF NATURAL HISTORY.

new houses were erected above the old, tier on tier, until they attained heights of three or more stories. Each story was stepped back from the one below to allow for a terrace on every floor.

Instead of roof hatches, the upper-level houses had doors leading out onto the terraces, which were reached by a succession of ladders. Sometimes they also had small windows covered with selenite. Selenite is a clear variety of gypsum that splits easily into layers. Slabs of it about an inch thick were fitted carefully into the windows and held in place with sticks.

The Catal Huyuk style of building gradually died out in the Middle East as towns spread beyond their old boundaries and blossomed into cities. No longer were houses jumbled together in a single mass. Now they were laid out along alleys, streets, or boulevards, and the entire city was usually surrounded by a separate defensive wall.

Within the city wall people lived much more comfortably than before. By 2000 B.C. the courtyard, or patio, house had been developed in the city of Ur in Mesopotamia. Although this type of house, like those at Catal Huyuk, had no windows facing the street, it was filled with light. The house was built around a central courtyard. All the rooms in the house opened onto the courtyard and drew their light and air from it, through either doorways or small windows.

The courtyard house combined privacy and protection with pleasant outdoor living. Because it rarely got cold in the Middle East, the doors and windows could be left uncovered most of the time. Flowering plants and shrubs often grew in the courtyard, and the family's cooking was usually done there, too. Smoke rose from the central hearth and escaped to the sky much as it had through the roof openings in the dwellings of prehistoric times.

Palaces in Mesopotamia and other regions of the Middle East were simply bigger, more sprawling versions of the courtyard house. Instead of one courtyard, a palace might have three, four, or more. To provide additional light in the outer rooms, builders began to include exterior windows in their designs for palaces. But apparently these windows made some people nervous.

In a myth told in the land of Canaan, Baal, god of fertility and life, ordered his builders to construct for him a huge palace that would cover 24,000 acres. Although Baal objected, the builders insisted on including a large window in the palace's wall. As a result Mot, the god of sterility and death, was able to get into the palace and do great damage.

A similar fear of windows is conveyed by the words of the prophet Jeremiah in the Old Testament (Jeremiah 9:21). Jeremiah said: "For death is come up into our windows, and is entered into our palaces, to cut off the children from without, and the young men from the streets."

Why were ancient people so afraid of windows? We can't be sure, but there are several possible explanations. Streets in ancient cities were narrow, and at night they were almost completely dark. It would have been relatively easy for a thief to approach a house unseen, climb in through a window, steal valuables, and then flee down the dark street.

Disease was also a frightening and mysterious thing to the people of the ancient world, and they had little idea of

COURTESY OF THE METROPOLITAN MUSEUM OF ART, MUSEUM EXCAVATION, 1919–1920; ROGERS FUND, SUPPLEMENTED BY A CONTRIBUTION OF EDWARD S. HARKNESS.

Wooden model of a courtyard from a house in ancient Egypt. The model was made about 2000 B.C. and was found buried in a tomb at Thebes.

how various ailments were transmitted. Perhaps they thought sickness could drift into a house through an open window. If so, wouldn't they be safer if their homes had no openings onto the outside world?

Houses in ancient Egypt followed much the same pattern as houses elsewhere in the Middle East. A large living room and several smaller rooms faced a central courtyard from which they drew light and air. Mats woven in colorful geometric patterns hung over the doors and windows. The mats could be rolled up in fine weather and let down when the sun became too bright, or on those rare occasions when it rained.

Sandstone window grille from an ancient Egyptian palace.

In larger Egyptian houses the living room often had a higher ceiling than the surrounding rooms. This permitted windows to be cut into the upper living-room walls that rose above the rest of the house. Windows of this type are called *clerestories* because they are clear of the lower stories. Such high windows, which in Egypt were often covered with stucco grilles, allowed light and air to enter while at the same time maintaining the privacy of those inside.

Clerestory windows also appeared in the Egyptian temple to Amun, creator and father of all things, that was built at Karnak between 1991 and 1786 B.C. This temple, like Egyptian houses and smaller temples, had an outer court that was open to the sky. Beyond it came a great reception hall that was grander than almost any structure that had been built up to that time. Even today its ruins awe the thousands of tourists who visit Karnak.

The hall was 320 feet long by 160 feet wide. Down the center stretched lines of giant stone columns, six on each side of the aisle. These columns, which supported the central portion of the roof, were nearly 12 feet in diameter and rose to a height of 69 feet. Brightly colored paintings and hieroglyphic writing covered their surfaces.

On either side of the central aisle lay another columned area, each containing sixty pillars that were 9 feet in diameter and 42 feet high. Because the roof covering the central part of the hall was almost 30 feet higher than the roofs over the two lower areas, the upper walls of the main aisle could be pierced with large clerestory windows. The windows were covered with carved stone grilles.

It must have been a thrilling experience to leave the sunny courtyard and enter the mysterious, dimly lit hall. Here and there light from the high clerestory windows caught the colors on the richly painted columns and created patterns of light and shade on the stone floor. Meanwhile, the corners of the hall remained in deep shadow. And at the far end of the central aisle the sacred figures

Model of the main hall of the temple at Karnak showing its huge columns as they looked when they were new. The clerestory windows covered by grilles are visible above the lower columns at the right. Note scale of small human figure in a white robe at the bottom.

of the Egyptian gods stood in even deeper darkness.

A similar combination of light, mystery, and drama would be achieved centuries later in the great cathedrals of western Europe. But it was accomplished for the first time by the unknown architects who designed the clerestory windows in the temple at Karnak.

THREE

❖

Through Panes of Glass

While the Egyptians were building courtyard houses with few windows, the people of Crete, an island in the Mediterranean Sea, were constructing remarkably modern houses of four or five rooms, with large windows in each room. The foundations of hundreds of such houses have been unearthed in the ruins of Knossos, which was the capital city of Crete. They date from between 2000 and 1600 B.C., when the Cretan civilization was at its height.

Like many of the windows we have, the windows in Cretan houses and palaces were divided into squares by vertical wooden bars (which we call *mullions*) and horizontal bars (which are known as *transoms*). The squares themselves are called *panes* or *lights*. No one knows exactly what the

Cretans used to cover the panes in their windows. It was probably a translucent material such as mica or alabaster, since the art of glassblowing still hadn't been invented.

It's a mystery why the Cretans, unlike any other people in the ancient world, felt free to include large windows in the outside walls of their dwellings. They must have trusted one another. And they must have felt secure from attack by an invader on their rocky island. That probably explains why almost no remains of fortifications have been found around any of the major Cretan towns.

No invader ever did conquer Crete. Instead, the peaceful island was struck in about 1400 B.C. by a natural disaster, possibly an earthquake followed by fire. The Cretan civilization never recovered from this catastrophe. And it would be hundreds of years before any other people enjoyed homes like those of the Cretans with their airy, light-filled rooms.

Certainly the ancient Greeks on the mainland did not. They surrounded their cities with elaborate walls and fortifications, designed to protect the inhabitants against raids by an enemy. Most of the dwellings inside the walls were crude, windowless structures lit only by smoke holes in the roofs.

Later Greek cities followed the Mesopotamian and Egyptian pattern. Low, whitewashed houses faced inward on small courtyards and presented an almost solid wall to the street. If the houses had any exterior windows, they were small and high up in the wall.

The Greeks appreciated windows, however, and realized that they were similar in structure to the human eye. As an opening in the wall of a building, a window, like the eye, links the visible world of nature to the invisible world of the mind. The ancient Greeks expressed this thought in a poetic way when they called the eye "the window of the soul."

At the centers of their cities, the Greeks erected great temples like the Parthenon in Athens. Located atop a high, fortified place called the Acropolis, the Parthenon was built on a stepped stone platform 228 feet long and 101 feet wide. A *peristyle*, or row, of forty-six marble columns ran all around the temple, with eight at either end. These columns were each 34 feet tall. Construction of the Parthenon began in 447 B.C., and the building wasn't finished until fifteen years later, in 432 B.C.

Inside, in the central shrine of the Parthenon, stood a 33-foot-tall statue of Athena, the Greek goddess of wisdom. The goddess's face, hands, and feet were veneered with ivory. Gold plate covered her sculpted robes, and precious stones were set into her eye sockets. Behind Athena's shrine

Model of the Parthenon in Athens as historians imagine it looked when completed in the fifth century B.C.
COURTESY OF THE METROPOLITAN MUSEUM OF ART, PURCHASE, 1890, LEVI HALE WILLARD BEQUEST.

was another large room that contained the treasury of the Acropolis. This room may also have been the home of the young women who took care of the temple and guarded its sacred treasures.

Surprisingly for such a large structure, the Parthenon had no windows in its high stone walls. Was it without natural light then? There are three different theories about this. One suggests that a large, rectangular hole had been left in the roof directly above the statue of Athena. This seems unlikely, though, because there are no signs in the floor of any slant or drain for rainwater.

The second theory is that the roof of the Parthenon, and other Greek temples like it, had beams of timber covered with thin slabs of Persian marble or alabaster. Though not transparent, these slabs would have let in enough light to give the shrine a soft glow.

The third theory is that the huge eastern doors of the temple were left open all day. The sun's rays streamed through the doorway and shone directly on Athena's golden robes, providing all the light needed to illuminate her shrine.

We'll probably never know which theory is correct. The Parthenon has been roofless for centuries, and no written descriptions of its roof have survived either.

Ancient Roman houses centered on a courtyard called an *atrium*, from which the rooms drew most of their light. These houses, like those of the Greeks, had few if any windows in their exterior walls.

By the first century B.C., the atria in most Roman houses were completely open to the sky and often had pools in the center in which rainwater could be collected. But originally the atrium contained a central hearth fire, like the dwellings of prehistoric times. In fact, the word "atrium" is related to the Latin word for "black" because of the smoke that once discolored its walls before escaping through a hole in the roof.

Like the Greeks, the Romans built magnificent temples to their gods. One of the grandest and most unusual of these was the Pantheon, which still stands in the center of Rome today. Erected in the second century A.D. by the Emperor Hadrian and dedicated to the gods of the planets, the Pantheon is a circular temple over 142 feet in diameter.

Inside, the building rises to exactly the same height as its diameter. It is topped with a huge dome, which later served as the inspiration for the dome of the U.S. Capitol in Washington. In the center of the dome is a great open "eye," 27 feet across, which provides the only source of natural light for the temple. Beneath this opening, the floor slopes gently downward to a drain for rainwater.

There could be no windows in the Pantheon, even if the Romans had wanted them, because its masonry walls had to be twenty feet thick in order to support the enormous weight of the dome. But the Romans seemed content with the one great circular opening, which to them symbolized the sun. When the sky was clear, a strong beam of sunlight slanted downward into the temple and lighted its farthest corners. But if a cloud passed over, the great chamber suddenly and dramatically darkened, reminding the Romans of the sun's tremendous power.

As the population of Rome and other cities in the empire

grew, there wasn't room for everyone to have a sprawling private house with a courtyard in the center. To solve this space problem, the Romans began to build the world's first apartment houses. These were concrete structures of five or six stories, with shops on the ground floor and apartments of two or three rooms each on the floors above. Narrow stairways rose from floor to floor.

Some of the rooms in a typical apartment faced the street, others a courtyard or alley at the back. Whichever way they faced, the rooms on the upper floors came equipped with large windows. In poorer districts most of these windows were covered only with wooden shutters that kept out rain and the heat of the midday sun. Some of the windows had wooden frames over which were stretched oiled cloth or translucent *vellum*—thin sheets of calfskin or lambskin.

In more expensive apartment houses, people had windows made of mica or gypsum, some of which were transparent enough to see through. And beginning in the second century A.D., apartments in Rome and other cities began to feature windows with bronze frames and nine-by-twelve-inch panes of a wonderful new material—glass.

Hard yet fragile, glass can shatter in a second or survive for thousands of years. It is formed when a silica such as sand is heated with soda ash and lime in a furnace. At a temperature of about 1500° centigrade the powdery mixture

Interior of the Pantheon in Rome, showing great circular "eye" in the dome. Painting by Giovanni Paolo Pannini, 1691–1765.

*Reconstructed bedroom from a Roman villa near
the town of Boscoreale, circa 40–30* B.C.
*The couch, footstool, window frame, wall paintings,
and mosaic floor are all authentically Roman.*

*Wall painting of Roman balconies and windows
from the villa bedroom at Boscoreale.*

liquifies into a cherry-red substance that resembles molten lava.

No one knows who actually invented glass more than 3000 years ago. The Roman historian Pliny credited the discovery to sailors from the country of Phoenicia. According to Pliny, the sailors landed on a beach along the Mediterranean Sea, propped up a cooking pot on some blocks of natron, a soda, that they were carrying as cargo, and built a fire to cook their evening meal. To the sailors' surprise, the sand beneath the fire melted and ran in a red-hot stream toward the water. As they looked on in amazement, the stream cooled and hardened into glass.

Few people believe Pliny's story today, but he may well have been right in thinking that someone in the Middle East discovered glassmaking by accident. What we do know is that by 1500 B.C. the people of Mesopotamia were stringing together necklaces made of glass beads. At about the same time the ancient Egyptians were making dishes and bottles of glass by winding threads of molten glass around a core of clay or by dipping a clay core into a pot of molten glass. But it wasn't until glassmakers perfected the art of glassblowing that the use of glass in windows became a possibility.

Glass was probably blown for the first time about 50 B.C. somewhere along the coast of Syria or Palestine, which was then part of the Roman Empire. In the blowing process a glassmaker took up a blob, or *gather*, of hot, molten glass on the end of a tube called an *iron*. He blew through the tube and inflated the glass into a bubble that he could work into a great variety of sizes and shapes. To make glass for windows, he blew the bubble into a cylindrical shape and cut off the ends. Then he split the cylinder lengthwise with a hot iron, reheated it, and flattened it out into a sheet of glass.

The secret of making blown glass spread quickly throughout the Roman Empire. A new profession, that of the *glazier*, came into being to meet the demand for window glass. Roman glaziers not only sold glass but cut the panes to the proper size and fitted them into window frames.

Besides installing glass windows in the new apartment blocks they were building, the Romans used them in the great public baths that were so popular in Roman cities and beach resorts. Glass windows not only kept in the steamy heat the baths generated but provided light and allowed patrons to look out on the landscape.

The writer Seneca might have been describing a modern resort when he wrote these words about Roman seaside baths: "Today we call baths louseholes if they are not designed to attract the sun all day through large windows, unless men can bathe and acquire a suntan simultaneously, and unless they have a view over the countryside and the sea from their indoor pools."

Glass windows were especially prized in the far northern regions of the Roman Empire, such as France and Britain, where winters were long, dark, and cold. There builders constructed two-story villas for wealthy Roman officials. The villas had massive oak doors and timber and stucco walls that were often two feet thick. On the ground floors of these houses the windows were usually small and set high in the walls for security's sake. But those on the upper floors were made as large as possible, especially the ones that faced south and caught the most sunlight. We know these windows were glazed because fragments of glass, some still in their frames, have been found buried in the ruins of Roman houses at Chichester and other places in England.

When the Roman Empire was at its height in the second century A.D., glass ceased being a luxury product. Glass-blowers were hard at work in Roman outposts from Britain in the West to Mesopotamia in the East. They produced thousands upon thousands of beads, dishes, bottles, and panes for windows.

But this vast industry died out almost entirely as one part of the Empire after another fell to attacks by barbarian tribes in the fourth and fifth centuries A.D. The attackers looted the villas of the Romans, shattered their windows, and often burned the houses to the ground. If they had any windows at all in their own dwellings, the conquerors went back to covering them with linen, animal skins, or simply wooden shutters.

Meanwhile, a new type of window covering had come into use on the other side of the world, in China and Japan. It was a material that we think of as common today, but that wasn't yet known in the West. What was it? Paper.

FOUR

❖

Where House and Garden Were One

Roman traders carried glass dishes and vases as far as China. There a poet, writing in the third century A.D., compared the beauty of glass to a spring day, and its clearness to winter ice.

But the Chinese themselves made few objects out of glass, and probably didn't learn glassblowing techniques until the 1600s. They didn't need to as far as window coverings were concerned. For sometime in the first century A.D., the Chinese had discovered paper, a material that served their purposes much better.

The invention of paper is credited to Ts'ai Lun, a guard in the court of the Chinese emperor. As the story goes, Ts'ai Lun and his fellow guards were trying to find a use for waste scraps of silk from the emperor's silk-making

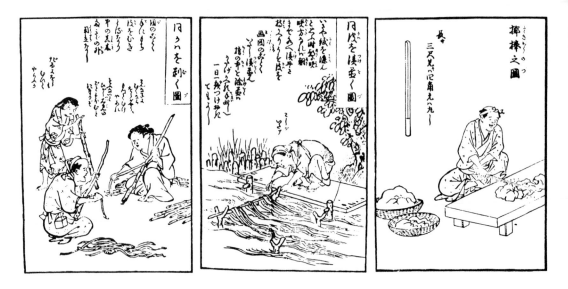

workshop. They took the scraps, beat them, and threw them into a pond to soften them further. As the fibers rose to the surface of the water, Ts'ai Lun had an idea. He captured the fibers on a fine screen, evened them out, and left them to dry in the sun. Thus the first sheet of paper was created.

Within a few years craftsmen throughout China were making paper. They discovered that many different raw materials could be used—the bark of trees, plant stems, old rags—as long as they contained the necessary cellulose. With each raw material the process was the same: After the material had been beaten to a pulp, it was mixed with water in a vat, then lifted from the water on a sievelike screen, as Ts'ai Lun had done. When the water drained off, a thin sheet of matted fiber, or paper, remained on the screen. This sheet was then pressed flat and stuck on a heated wall like a poster until it was thoroughly dry.

At first the Chinese used the new material mainly as a surface for writing. It was light, so it could be carried easily

Steps in papermaking, from a Japanese woodcut, 1798.

from place to place, and its thinness and flatness made it ideal for storing. But the Chinese soon realized that paper had other desirable qualities. Although thin, it proved to be surprisingly durable. And it was translucent, which meant it could be used as a covering for windows.

The architectural style the Chinese had developed was perfectly suited to paper-covered windows. For, like the ancient Egyptians and Greeks, the Chinese surrounded their houses and palaces with walls, and all the windows opened onto safe, secure inner courtyards or gardens. South-facing rooms, which got the most sunshine in winter, were occupied by the older members of the family. Rooms in the east and west sides of the courtyard were for children and guests. A wall containing a gate to the street usually formed the south side of the structure.

The reasons for this layout—and for the layouts of Chinese cities as a whole—had their roots in ancient Chinese mythology. According to these myths, south is the direction of the vermilion bird of summer, and is the source of fire and life. North is the direction of the tortoise and the snake, and is associated with winter and death. Believing this, Chinese builders of houses, palaces, and temples tried to have as many windows as possible face south, the life-giving direction.

The courtyard garden was more than just a garden to a Chinese family. It was almost like another room of the house, and the owners wanted everyone to have a good view of it through his or her window.

In a poor city household the courtyard might be tiny, but even so there would be a few potted plants in it. In a wealthy home the walled garden was often larger than the house. In fact a poet of the T'ang period (A.D. 618–907) recommended that in a well-planned residence, half of the space should be devoted to man-made hills, ponds, and streams; a third to flower beds, bamboo groves, and trees; and only a sixth to the house itself.

Because the garden was so important, the walls that faced it were left as open as possible. Sliding doors led out onto verandas beneath the overhanging eaves of the tiled roof. Often the doors were not solid but were composed of wooden grilles set in frames. Craftsmen carved the grilles in elaborate patterns from a hard wood such as gingko and covered them with a fine paper made from the stems of rice plants.

Next to the doors, the brick wall of the house rose to a height of only about twenty inches above ground level. This allowed for large windows to fill the rest of the wall. Like the doors, the windows were usually covered with decorative wooden grilles.

A Chinese village at Spring Festival time, showing houses with courtyards and paper-covered windows. Painted-silk hand scroll from the Ming Dynasty (1368– 1644).

In southern China, where the weather stayed warm almost all year, the doors and windows were left open most of the time. The low-hanging eaves of the roof shielded the rooms in the house from rains and shaded them against the afternoon sun. Meanwhile, with both doors and windows open, it was almost as if the house and garden were one.

In northern China, where the winters could turn bitter cold, the doors and windows had to remain closed for half the year. Their paper coverings were coated with oil to help them withstand the strong winds of winter.

Even in the north, though, window and door openings were made as large as possible in order to admit light into the house. The roof tiles at the ends of the eaves curved upward so that the rays of the sun would reach into the

A Chinese family of the early 1900s enjoys the fresh air in their Peking courtyard. Behind them are paper-covered windows with elaborate wooden frames.

farthest corners of the rooms. And on fine days in spring and summer, people in northern China, like those in the south, flung open their doors and windows so they could delight in the beauty of their gardens.

The knowledge of how to make paper reached Japan from China early in the seventh century A.D. As they had with other Chinese crafts and customs, the Japanese quickly mastered papermaking and adapted it to their own architecture.

Like the Chinese, the Japanese prized gardens. A Japanese

family would surround its garden with high walls to insure privacy and build wide verandas along all the sides of the house that faced it. There the family could sit under the protecting eaves and look out at the rock pool and the carefully arranged clusters of flowers, shrubs, and trees.

When the Japanese introduced paper into the construction of their houses, they used it even more widely than the Chinese. On two or more sides of a house they did away completely with permanent walls and substituted sliding wooden panels called *shoji*, which they covered with high quality paper.

Inside the house there were few solid partitions, either. In their place, the Japanese put paper-covered screens called *fusuma* that slid back and forth in grooves in the floor and ceiling. This type of lightweight construction was possible because the walls in a Japanese house, like those in Chinese houses, did not help to support the tiled roof. Its weight was carried entirely by wooden posts driven deep into the foundation.

The interior screens, the fusuma, could be opened to make larger rooms or removed entirely to create a single huge space. The frame of a fusuma consisted of a grating made of thin strips of wood. Thick sheets of paper were glued on both sides of the grating, and in richer homes artists often painted colorful landscapes directly on the paper.

Like the fusuma, the shoji in the outer walls were made of light wooden bars that crisscrossed each other, leaving rectangular openings. The openings couldn't be more than ten inches wide, because that was the width of the rolls of rice paper that were used to cover the frame. The paper was pasted over the outside of the frame only, so that more light would enter the house on cloudy days. In fine weather, the whole side wall of the house could be slid back, flooding the rooms with sunlight and bringing the garden inside.

To protect the shoji against heavy rains and violent autumn storms, the Japanese covered all but the smallest windows with wooden rain shutters. These slid in grooves like the screens themselves and disappeared into compartments at the sides of the shoji when not in use. It became the Japanese custom to close the shutters at sunset and open them again at dawn when a new day began.

The Japanese also took steps to protect the paper-covered shoji from damage by people. A foot-high wooden panel was usually included at the bottom of every shoji in case someone accidentally kicked it. And the Japanese, who traditionally sat on woven floor mats rather than chairs, were careful never to sit too close to a shoji or fusuma. They were afraid they might lean against it without thinking and break through the paper covering.

Even with all these precautions, the shoji paper got dirty in time and small holes appeared in it. Most Japanese families changed the panels every six months, once in the spring and again in the autumn. Repairmen could be hired to do the job, but many Japanese repapered the shoji screens themselves. They made a family project of it, with children helping their parents and learning the skill.

While the Chinese and Japanese were perfecting their

House in Kyoto, Japan, with overhanging eaves and paper-covered windows and doors.

COURTESY OF JAPAN NATIONAL
TOURIST ORGANIZATION.

A Japanese mother and her children watch the full moon rise through open shoji *screens.*

COURTESY OF JAPAN NATIONAL
TOURIST ORGANIZATION.

Three people wearing traditional Japanese clothing take part in the tea ceremony in a room with paper-covered windows.

use of paper in windows, people in the west still covered the windows in their homes with cloth or vellum. Paper mills weren't established in Italy until the 1200s, in France and Germany until the 1300s, and in England until the later 1400s.

By then, hundreds of years had passed since the fall of the Roman Empire, and agriculture, trade, and architecture had begun to revive in western Europe. But the glass industry was still in a primitive state, and even powerful kings and barons usually had no glass in their windows.

There was only one exception to this gloomy pattern. Great cathedrals were rising in France and other European countries. To add to their beauty and majesty, church builders began to make a new kind of window. They put together pieces of colored glass and created the marvels known as stained-glass windows.

FIVE

❖

Miracles of Color and Light

One morning in the year 1144, Abbé Suger, head of the monastery of St. Denis near Paris, entered the monastery's newly rebuilt church. He walked slowly toward the chancel at the eastern end of the church, where light streamed in through tall stained-glass windows.

As he stood admiring the beautiful patterns in the glass, Suger was pleased. Like most Christians, he believed that light was a direct link between human beings on earth and the spirit of God in heaven. Consequently, he had instructed the architects to make sure "that the whole church be resplendent with a marvelous, uninterrupted light, radiating from windows of maximum luminosity." Now, as he looked about him, Suger saw that the architects had gone far beyond his instructions and achieved a beauty even he could not have imagined. Truly, he thought, they must have been inspired by God.

The new windows of St. Denis soon inspired thousands of others. On foot, by boat, and on horseback, these pilgrims journeyed to Paris from all over France to visit St. Denis, the monastery where every French king since the seventh century was buried. They worshipped in the new church and marveled at its windows with their glowing scenes from the life of Jesus and his mother, Mary. And they returned home determined to replace their own dark, thick-walled churches with new ones similar to St. Denis.

The time was ripe for a wave of church building, not only in France but throughout western Europe. In the 700 years since the fall of the Roman Empire, the Roman Catholic Church had become more and more powerful. By the 1100s it possessed the economic strength to finance the construction of great cathedrals in cities large and small.

At the same time, builders were perfecting a new style of architecture, the Gothic, that permitted the construction of much taller and lighter churches. In place of the rounded arches of the earlier Romanesque style (so named because it resembled the architecture of the Roman Empire), the new Gothic arches were pointed and could reach higher.

The roofs in Gothic churches were not supported by thick stone or masonry walls, as in Romanesque churches, but by stone piers or columns, spaced evenly along the sides of the building. As a result, the stretches of wall between the piers did not have to be thick, and large areas could be left open for windows.

The church of St. Denis, like the other churches and cathedrals that followed it, was built in the shape of a cross to remind worshippers of the cross upon which Jesus was crucified. Each of its four corners, and the windows in them, had a special symbolic meaning.

The long central section of the church, the nave, ran from west to east, with the main entrance at the western end and the chancel with its altar at the eastern end. Thus a worshipper walking into the church for a morning service would see the chancel bathed in light from the rising sun.

The morning sun meant life to the people of the Middle Ages, so the stained-glass windows in the chancel often portrayed scenes from the life of Christ and the miracles he performed. At the opposite end of the church, the setting sun of late afternoon made people think of old age and death. So the windows above the western entrance often showed a tableau of the Last Judgment, when it was decided whether a person would go to heaven or hell.

Crossing the nave at right angles and extending from north to south was the shorter arm of the cross. It was called the transept. In the Middle Ages the northern end of the transept symbolized the Old Testament. The stained glass in its windows was largely blue, the color of the cold north, and it dramatized episodes from the lives of the Old Testament prophets and judges.

Opposite these windows, at the southern end of the transept, were panels of red and orange glass that symbolized the New Testament. A warm, cheerful light spilled through the southern windows at noon on sunny days. It reminded worshippers of the promise of salvation the

New Testament contained and made them feel hopeful.

Narrow, sharply pointed windows called lancets ran along both sides of the nave. Their stained-glass panels often depicted scenes from the lives of the saints. These, like the windows in the other parts of the church, helped to tell the familiar stories of the Bible and the Catholic Church to a large public, most of whom could not read.

Tucked away in the corners of many windows were portraits in glass of the people who had contributed to the construction of the cathedral. The king and his elegant queen were usually there, along with the wealthy barons of the land, the bishops of the church, and the powerful knights in their armor. So were the humbler people who had given money: cloth merchants, weavers, water carriers. And those who had actually built the church were there, too: the stonecutters, masons, and glassmakers.

No one knows exactly when stained glass was first made or where. Some examples of colored glass that probably date back to the 700s have been found in France. But it wasn't manufactured in a widespread way until the 1100s, the century when the church of St. Denis was rebuilt.

Many of the glassworks were connected with monasteries and supplied the needs of their churches and others in the surrounding area. The techniques of making stained glass, known as *metal* in its molten state, were comparatively

View down the Gothic-style nave of Worcester Cathedral, England.
COURTESY OF THE BRITISH TOURIST AUTHORITY.

simple and changed little over the years. To color the glass, craftsmen added various metallic oxides to pots of the liquid material. As a result, the colored glass was called pot metal. Cobalt produced a beautiful blue glass, while iron produced a vivid red and copper a deep green.

Next the glassmakers blew the molten glass into cylinders, as the Romans had done, cut them down the middle, and opened them out into flat sheets. Or else they transferred the molten bubble to an iron rod and spun the bubble until it spread itself into a large, flat disk. Both of these glass-making methods were widely used in medieval Europe.

With a stock of colored glass on hand, the glazier could begin the process of making a window. He started by drawing a sketch of the overall design for approval by the church officials. Once the design was agreed upon, he drew it full size on a wooden tabletop that had been whitened with chalk or whitewash. If the glazier was making a large window, he could draw only one or two sections at a time. His drawing was called a *cartoon*.

On the cartoon, the glazier sketched in all the details of facial features, clothing, and background that would appear on the window. He also indicated where and how the individual pieces of glass would fit and what colors they would be. When the cartoon was finished, it looked like the drawing for a jigsaw puzzle.

The glazier then took a sheet of colored glass—say red—and laid it over the cartoon. On the upper surface of the glass he traced the outlines of all the red pieces that would be required for the window. He cut the glass with a tool called a *grozing iron* that looked like a metal pencil. After

Scene from the life of Saint Nicholas, made with pot-metal glass. From a cathedral, in the French city of Soissons, built between 1210 and 1215.

Rose window from Notre Dame Cathedral, Paris, showing elaborate stone tracery.

Coat of arms of the German Emperor Maximilian I, surrounded by tournament scenes. Made of pot-metal glass and white glass, painted with silver stain. From the city of Nuremberg, circa 1486–1490.

This window in two parts depicts the angel, on the left, coming to tell the Virgin Mary, on the right, that she will give birth to Jesus Christ. Made in Florence, Italy, in the 1400s by Giovanni di Domenico, it is a good example of later stained-glass windows where artists painted their designs directly on clear glass with enamels.

Window with magnolia blossoms and irises by Louis Comfort Tiffany and the Tiffany Studios, circa 1905.

"Peony in the Wind" by John La Farge. Window from the John Hay House, Washington, D.C., circa 1893. Photograph by Margaret Harman.

*Grapevine window by the Tiffany Studios,
circa 1902.*

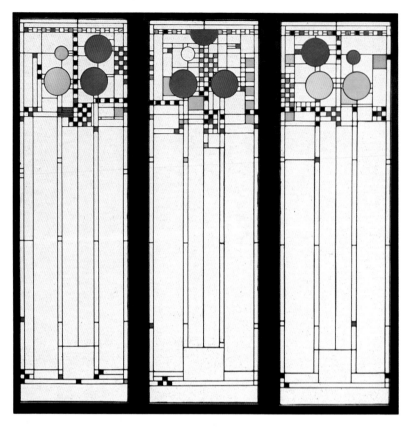

*Trio of windows by Frank Lloyd Wright from the Avery Coonley Playhouse,
Riverside, Illinois, 1912. Note miniature American flag in window at left.*

A glazier paints a design on a piece of glass. Woodcut by Jost Amman, Frankfurt, 1568.

heating the sharp end of the iron, he passed it slowly along the trace lines on the glass, then cracked the glass by cooling the heated parts with cold water. He repeated this process with each sheet of colored glass until he had cut out all the pieces he needed.

He put the pieces in their proper positions and, staring through the glass, carefully painted on their surfaces the details and shadings he could see on the cartoon below. He

The glazier fastens the panes of a window together with lead cames on his worktable. Another woodcut by Jost Amman, Frankfurt, 1568.

used a special dark-brown enamel that looked black or gray when seen against the light. Because of this, it was called *grisaille, gris* being the French word for gray.

The painted pieces of glass were fired in a kiln so that the enamel would adhere permanently to the surfaces. Then they were ready to be assembled in a panel. To do this, the glazier and his assistants arranged them on the table again and surrounded them with flexible pieces of lead called *cames*. The cames could easily be bent, and they had grooves on either side so that adjacent pieces of glass could be fitted neatly into them.

After making sure all the cames were properly aligned, the glazier and his helpers soldered them to one another with a hot iron and made the joints waterproof with putty. In a well-designed window, the black lines of the cames contributed to the overall pattern and helped to give it form and balance.

When all the panels for a stained-glass window were finished, they were transported to the building site and inserted into the window opening. In narrow openings, horizontal iron supports called *saddle bars* were enough to hold the individual panels in place. But in wider windows, vertical iron posts provided additional support. Window designers took the bars and posts into account and used them to frame the individual scenes in the Bible stories the windows dramatized. The effect was almost like that of the divisions in a modern-day comic strip.

Workers had to climb high up on wooden scaffolding to solder the window panels onto the iron supports. It was hard, dangerous work, and it became even more so when architects began to build taller and bigger cathedrals, with larger window areas.

The invention of the *flying buttress* speeded this development. Before then, the pillars and posts that supported cathedral roofs had been aligned with the wall and were usually a part of it. The flying buttress, on the other hand, arched away from the wall like a wing and reached the ground at a point eight or more feet distant.

The additional support the flying buttress provided enabled church builders to raise the nave higher and make the walls thinner. The nave of Notre Dame Cathedral in Paris, completed in 1253, rose to an unprecedented height of 110 feet, and the windows in the side walls were 32 feet tall. Even taller were the stained-glass windows in the nave of Chartres Cathedral, built at about the same time as Notre Dame. They stretched upward to a hight of 46 feet and were described by one observer as looking like "a series of glowing banners hung upon the walls."

As the windows in the great cathedrals grew taller and wider, the old-style framework of metal bars and posts was no longer strong enough to carry the weight of the glass panels. It became necessary to subdivide the window area, which was often fifteen or more feet wide, into two or three sections. These sections were separated by stone bars that were carved as thin as possible so they wouldn't interfere with the design of the window.

Stone bars, or *tracery*, as it was called, were also used in the great circular rose windows that appeared above the main and side entrances of Gothic cathedrals. It was only natural for the architects to include rose windows in their plans, since the rose was the emblem of the Virgin Mary and symbolized her love and mercy.

The rose windows in Notre Dame Cathedral, which was dedicated to Mary, "Our Lady," were especially spectacular. The one above the western entrance, completed in 1225,

Rear view of Notre Dame Cathedral, Paris, showing flying buttresses.

shone with an abundance of royal-blue glass and was 32 feet in diameter. Those in the transept, above the northern and southern entrances, were installed later and extended to an amazing diameter of 43 feet.

It was, and is, an exhilarating experience to stand in the middle of Notre Dame and look from one rose window to another. As a French expert on art and architecture said, "The vanished wall has made for wheels of fire . . . which recall the wheels of the most ancient folklore, emblems of the sun. All is combined here to satisfy the eye and the mind at the same time."

The grand climax of Gothic church windows was still ahead, however. It came in the mid-1200s with the construction in Paris of Sainte-Chapelle, a royal chapel built to house the crown of thorns that Jesus had supposedly worn when he was crucified.

The upper chapel of Sainte-Chapelle was tall and without side aisles. Its stained-glass windows covered virtually all the wall areas and reached from near the floor almost to the ceiling. On sunny days the delicate stone tracery that held together the dazzling panels of blue and ruby glass seemed to disappear. At those times visitors to Sainte-Chapelle felt as if they were in an enchanted room made of nothing but color and light.

SIX

❖

Slits in Castle Walls

While architects of the 1200s and 1300s were including larger and larger windows in cathedrals, wealthy European nobles lived in castles with openings in the walls that were more like slits than windows.

The typical French or English castle of the time was surrounded first by a moat and then by high walls with a heavily guarded gate through which visitors entered. At the center of the castle stood a towerlike stone structure called the keep. It was usually rectangular and had walls up to 20 feet thick. Some English keeps rose to heights of 60 feet or more.

The ground floor of the keep usually consisted of storerooms. They were lit only by uncovered slits in the stone walls that were deliberately made too narrow for even the thinnest enemy to squeeze through. The second floor served as living quarters for guards and servants, and it, too, had mere slits for windows. Above, on the third floor, was the great hall of the castle where the noble and his family held court.

The great hall was often two stories high, with a balcony circling it on the upper level. The lower level had slits in the wall like the rooms on the floors below. But the upper level, which was too high for an attacker to reach by ladder, usually had tall, narrow windows.

In the twelfth century, the windows in the great hall were

Keep of an eleventh-century Norman castle in Essex, England, with slitlike openings on the lower floors and larger windows above.
COURTESY OF THE BRITISH TOURIST AUTHORITY.

covered only with thick wooden shutters secured by iron bars. Sometimes the hall contained three or more huge fireplaces. It took that many to heat it in winter, when the shutters on the windows were opened and a cold wind swept into the hall along with the light.

Shuttered openings such as these helped to give us the word "window," which literally means "wind's eye." How better to describe an eye on the world through which the wind blew when it was open!

By the thirteenth century, an especially wealthy lord or baron might have glass in some of his windows. It was rare, though, for anyone to have windows made entirely of glass, because the material was still so expensive. Often only the top half or third of the window was fitted with small panes, held in place by strips of lead like the stained glass in church windows. A wooden shutter, which could be opened in good weather, covered the bottom part.

Glass windows became more common in castles in the fourteenth century, but they were still a luxury. Since many barons and nobles owned several castles, which they lived in at different times of the year, they devised a way to avoid the expense of outfitting all of them with glass windows. They had special window frames made that could be removed easily. When they traveled from one castle to another, the nobles and barons simply took their windows with them. Shutters kept out the wind and rain while they were away.

Great three-sided bay windows called *oriels* were added to the upper floors of many castles in the fourteenth century. They were big enough to sit in, and some even had fireplaces.

One such oriel, in Scotland's Stirling Castle, served an unusual purpose when King Edward I of England besieged the castle in 1304: Every morning the queen of Scotland and her ladies-in-waiting climbed up to the oriel and sat on cushioned seats to watch the fighting below.

During the twelfth and thirteenth centuries, many peasant families in England and western Europe lived in smoke-filled wooden huts without windows or even openings in the thatched roofs. The only light and ventilation came through the entrances. Sometimes these were covered with crudely made wooden doors, but more often with just woven cloth hangings.

It wasn't until the fourteenth century that prosperous peasants began to build a sturdier kind of cottage of wood and plaster. At the front there was usually only one window. It had no glass in it, but might be glazed instead with thin parchment or oiled linen. Or it might be covered by a single shutter hinged at the top, perhaps with leather thongs. In good weather the shutter could be raised and held open by a stick placed between it and the windowsill.

European towns and cities grew at a rapid rate in the thirteenth and fourteenth centuries as trade expanded and master craftsmen formed associations called guilds. Land in cities became more expensive, and few town houses were more than 25 feet wide. Often there was a shop on the ground floor and rooms for the owner of the house and his family on the floors above.

Before glass came into common use, most of the windows in town houses were glazed with thin pieces of animal horn, oiled paper, or cloth. The cloth was often dyed green or black because it was felt that white coverings disturbed one's sight. As a writer of the time said, "Black cloth does less harm to the eyes, is thicker against the wind, more difficult to see through, and keeps its color better."

To provide for light and ventilation, windows in town houses usually had two or three sections like the windows in castles. At the top was a glazed panel that was fixed in

Dooryard of a Dutch village house. Windows with small-paned glass sections can be seen above wooden shutters. Painting by Adriaen van Ostade, 1610–1685.
COURTESY OF THE NATIONAL GALLERY OF ART, WASHINGTON.

place and always remained shut. Below it were one or two hinged shutters that could be opened in good weather. In regions where the winters were very cold, windows sometimes came equipped with two sets of shutters, one of which swung out into the street and the other into the room.

When richer merchants and craftsmen began to install glass in their windows in the fourteenth century, they usually put it in the immovable upper sections, above the shutters. The glass came in small square or diamond-shaped pieces, and was called "white glass" because it was supposed to be clear.

A few wealthy merchants and town officials even had a pane or two of stained glass set into their front windows. These might illustrate the family's coat-of-arms or the sign of the Zodiac under which the head of the household was born. Because such a pane was a mark of prestige, it was often installed in a bay window overlooking the street, where it could be admired by passersby.

In the 1300s and 1400s, town houses in Paris and other European cities had no indoor plumbing. It was common practice then to empty chamber pots into the gutter from the windows of the upper floors. "Watch out for the water!" a French housewife would shout as a warning to pedestrians before dumping the contents of her pot. As a result of this practice, the stench in the streets was terrible, especially in summer, and the front windows of even the wealthiest homes had to be kept shut on hot days.

People living in the Moslem lands of the Middle East, North Africa, and southern Spain had a different problem with heat, and they built a different kind of window to

The great dining hall in Sulgrave Manor, the ancestral home of George Washington's family, in Northamptonshire, England. Note stained-glass panels in the windows.

help solve it. In these countries, where a hot sun blazed down for much of the year, people wanted to keep direct sunlight out of their homes while still allowing light to enter. To accomplish this, Moslem architects developed an unusual type of window that they usually left uncovered with glass or any other material.

The window consisted of a rectangular framework of wood or stucco that jutted out from the wall of a house. Its three sides were filled entirely with an elaborate grillwork

Moslem-style window in southern Spain, covered with a wooden grille.

of wood, cement, or iron. Looking out through the grille, a person could see up, down, or across the street without being observed. This was especially important for the women of the household, since Moslems believe that a woman's face should never be seen in public.

Meanwhile, church builders throughout western Europe were designing new and more colorful stained-glass windows during the 1300s and 1400s.

About 1325, stained-glass makers discovered that they could get a brilliant yellow if they painted the surface of clear glass with a silver oxide. According to legend, this happened accidentally when a worker's silver button came loose from his jacket, fell onto the sheet of glass he was blowing, and stained it yellow. Glassmakers also discovered that the longer the painted glass was fired in an oven, the more golden it became.

Now glaziers had a second color to work with besides black. Soon they developed others—a mossy green, a rich purple, and a reddish enamel that was perfect for flesh tones. No longer did glaziers have to cut out pieces of colored glass in the complicated shapes required. Instead they had a whole palette of colors that they could paint directly onto rectangles of white glass as if they were painting on wood, canvas, or paper.

To meet the demand for stained glass, the number of glaziers at work in England and other European countries increased enormously. They were found now not only in cities and large towns but even in villages. In 1364, English glaziers formed a guild to regulate the rules and standards of their work, and a royal glazier to the king of England was appointed in 1393.

All this success and recognition came to a sudden end in the 1500s. In Germany, a priest named Martin Luther challenged the authority of the Roman Catholic Church and led a revolt against it. This movement was known as the Protestant Reformation, and among its targets were all the saints whose lives had been portrayed in stained-glass windows.

In England at about the same time, King Henry VIII, who had been a Catholic, divorced his wife, Queen Catherine of Aragon, and broke with the Roman Catholic Church when it refused to accept his action. Between 1536 and

The ruins of Fountains Abbey in England, destroyed as a result of King Henry VIII's order.

1540 all Catholic monasteries in England were closed at the king's orders and their buildings, furnishings, and money seized. In place of the Catholic Church Henry established his own Church of England. And he decreed that henceforth there would be no images of saints or other Catholic religious figures in any English church.

As a result of Henry's decree, English makers of stained glass lost their most important source of work and income. Even worse, the decree marked the first step in a wave of destruction of church windows, not only in England but throughout western Europe.

SEVEN

❖

Windows That Went Up and Down

People in England loved the stained-glass windows in their churches, and many ignored King Henry VIII's orders to remove them. Recognizing this, Henry's son, King Edward VI, issued an even stronger decree in 1547. He ordered that churchmen "take away and destroy all shrines, pictures, paintings, and all other monuments of feigned miracles, idolatry, and superstition so there remain no memory of the same in walls, glass windows, or elsewhere within their churches or houses."

Still many people resisted the king's decree. They took the stained-glass panels out of the windows and replaced them with plain glass. But they didn't destroy the panels. Instead they hid them in barns and other places, hoping a time would come when they could return them to their frames.

Attacks on windows weren't limited to England. In France in 1562, Protestant followers of the religious leader John Calvin occupied the cities of Le Mans, Lyons, and Poitiers. They took over all Roman Catholic churches, carried off their treasures, and smashed their stained-glass windows. Later, after the occupation ended, Catholics sometimes managed to reconstruct a single window from fragments of eight or ten that had been shattered.

Back in England, Oliver Cromwell declared war once again on stained-glass windows in 1649. Cromwell was the leader of the Puritan forces that defeated and beheaded King Charles I. The Puritans got their name because they wanted to "purify" the Church of England of what they considered ungodly practices. Among other things, they feared that people might forget the true meaning of God if they looked at beautiful windows when they were in church. So they ordered their immediate destruction.

As in King Edward's time, many Englishmen removed their stained-glass windows before the Puritans could harm them. In some places, such as the city of York, the citizens stood up to angry Puritan mobs and managed to save the precious glass panels. In other places the upper windows in churches survived because they were too high for the Puritans to reach with their clubs and axes.

Stained-glass making didn't revive in England until 1660, when Oliver Cromwell's government was overthrown and King Charles II gained the throne. In the meantime, glass-

Empty windows in the ruins of Tintern Abbey, Wales.
COURTESY OF THE BRITISH TOURIST AUTHORITY.

makers in England and other European countries kept busy trying to meet the increased demand for plain window glass.

During the sixteenth and seventeenth centuries most northern European glass was made in forest glasshouses. Some of these were large settlements complete with cottages for the workers and manor houses for the owners. Others were small enterprises located near monasteries or the estates of noblemen. Whether large or small, the glasshouses had to be in forests because of the huge amounts of wood needed for fuel in the glassmaking process.

The glasshouses were run by families or guilds that made sure outsiders didn't learn their secrets. "Nobody shall teach glassmaking," said one owner, "to anyone whose father has not known glassmaking." Boys entered the craft as apprentices at the age of twelve and had to swear never to show "the noble art, usage, and science of glassmaking" to anyone outside the guild.

Glassmaking was hard, dangerous work. One writer in 1713 described it in these words: "During the process of making glass the men stand continually half-naked even in freezing winter weather near very hot furnaces, and keep their eyes fixed on the fire and the molten glass. Their eyes have to meet the full force of the fire. In time they shrivel because their nature and substance is burnt up and destroyed by the excessive heat."

In an attempt to protect himself, the forest glassmaker sometimes wore clothes and a hood or mask that were made from the skins of wild animals. Even so, his face and hands were usually black with soot from the fire. Their appearance made glassmakers so frightening a sight that

Forest glassmakers at work. At the top, they mix sand, soda ash, and lime in a pit. The mixture is heated in a furnace in the hut below, where a master craftsman can be seen blowing the molten glass into a bubble on the end of his pipe. Illustration from a late-fifteenth-century Austrian manuscript.

children often thought they were monsters and ran from them in terror.

The chief products of European glassmakers were drinking vessels and glass for windowpanes. The sand they used contained iron, which gave the glass a greenish tint. Only in the late 1500s did glassmakers finally learn how to make colorless glass, which was much better for windows.

Some glassmakers of the time decorated the vessels they made with designs cut into the surfaces by a pointed tool with a diamond on the end. And some English poets used the tool to engrave stanzas from their poems on window-panes. They gave the panes to their sweethearts as tokens of their love.

By the 1500s internal political conditions in France, England, and other European countries had calmed down to the point where nobles and landowners no longer felt they had to live in fortresses. In the castles French nobles built in the valley of the Loire River between 1508 and 1520, there were no surrounding defensive walls, and lily ponds replaced the moats of old. Instead of narrow slits in the walls, these new castles boasted large windows that looked out upon terraces, lawns, and formal gardens.

To make the most of such views, French castle builders developed a new style of window that came to be known as the French, or casement, window. It was taller than it was wide, and sometimes extended all the way to the floor. If it did, it was called a "French door." Its two glazed wooden frames, or sashes, were hinged at the sides and usually swung inward into the room. On the ground floor one could step through the French door onto a porch or terrace. On upper floors, the doors frequently opened onto balconies.

Many of the French castles also featured windows that stuck up out of the sharply slanted roofs and were covered with roofs of their own. These were called dormer windows from the French word *dormir*, which means "to sleep." They

The Chateau of Chambord in the Loire Valley, France. Note dormer windows in the roof.

were given this name because they were designed to bring light and air into the small attic rooms where the children and servants of the family slept.

Like their French counterparts, English nobles of the 1500s had an urge to gaze out freely upon the world, and it was reflected in the great country houses they built for themselves. Although Longleat House, begun in 1553, was constructed around a courtyard, like a castle, the important rooms in the house all faced outward on the surrounding park. Hardwick Hall, built between 1590 and 1597, had even larger windows than Longleat. They were so large, in fact, that people of the time chanted: "Hardwick Hall, more glass than wall."

Longleat House, England.

A new type of room in English houses took advantage of these large windows. It was called the long gallery, and sometimes it ran the entire width of the house. On one side of the long gallery the walls were covered with paintings—often portraits of the family's noble ancestors. On the other, a line of tall casement windows looked out on lawns and flower gardens. When the sun slanted in through the windows and fell on the furniture and carpets in the center of the room, it created a lovely atmosphere in the long gallery.

Although the window areas in French castles and English

The long gallery in Sledmere House, England.

country houses grew ever larger in the 1500s, the panes in the windows remained small. Within each rectangle formed by vertical mullions and horizontal transoms, there might be two dozen or more squares or circles of glass, held together by pieces of lead. The individual panes were so small because the forest glassmakers of the time had not yet learned how to make large sheets of glass.

While the wealthy were installing glass windows in their homes, poorer people in England and most other European countries were still covering their windows with animal horn, parchment, or oiled paper. Only in Holland could peasants in the countryside and ordinary city dwellers afford glass windows.

Holland's unusual prosperity during the 1600s was due to a number of things. Probably the most important was the fact that a majority of the Dutch people felt as if they had a stake in the success of the country. Unlike England, France, and Spain, all of which were ruled by kings, Holland was a republic—the first in Europe. Most of its peasants owned their own land, and many of its merchants ran their own businesses in Holland's towns and cities.

The peak of Holland's power—its so-called Golden Age— lasted from the beginning to almost the end of the 1600s. In that period, Holland became the most advanced ship-building nation in the world and developed large naval, fishing, and merchant fleets. Its explorers founded colonies in Africa and Asia as well as America. Its largest city, Amsterdam, was a major center of international commerce and finance. And its artists, such as Rembrandt and Vermeer, were among the world's finest.

As the prestige and prosperity of their country grew, the Dutch built homes for themselves that reached new heights of attractiveness and comfort. City dwellers lived in houses made of brick and wood, which were lighter than stone and thus less likely to sink into the damp, boggy soil of Holland.

Because of limited space in Dutch towns and cities, the houses were extremely narrow, sometimes only one room wide. They were built one next to the other in a row along the street and usually shared common walls. These shared walls carried all the weight of the roofs and floors, so Dutch builders could pierce the front and back walls of the houses with large windows. At first the chief function of the window areas may have been to save weight, but they also allowed light to penetrate far into the deep, narrow interior. As a result, Dutch rooms were much more sunny and cheerful than those in other European town houses of the time.

Before the 1600s the upper parts of Dutch windows had fixed glass panes, and only the lower halves, which were solid wood, could be opened. Later the bottom sections, too, were glazed, and they swung open like casement windows. The light coming through these windows was controlled by interior wooden shutters and by a new device: window curtains. Curtains quickly became popular because they offered privacy from the street while permitting light to enter the room. They also served as an additional barrier against the cold in winter.

As the window openings in Dutch houses grew larger, it became more awkward to swing the panels open in the

Sunlight streams through the windows in a seventeenth-century Dutch town house. Painting by Pieter de Hooch, 1629–1683.

Narrow seventeenth-century houses in Amsterdam, Holland, many with large sash windows.

old way. They came too far into the room and took up too much space. So the Dutch invented a new kind of window: the sash or double-hung window whose two sections could be opened by sliding them up from the bottom or down from the top.

When open, a sash window provided almost as much ventilation as a casement window and saved a considerable amount of space. It was soon adopted throughout Holland but failed to gain acceptance in other European countries. The French, for example, called it the "guillotine window" because the downward movement of the bottom sash reminded them of the falling blade that was used in France to behead criminals.

However, the efficiency of the sash window appealed to the English, who soon installed it on a wide scale in their homes and public buildings. And when Dutch and English settlers established colonies on the North American continent in the 1600s, they brought the idea of the sash window with them.

EIGHT

❖

The Crystal Palaces

When British settlers first built dwellings at Plymouth, Massachusetts, in the 1620s, they were crudely made shelters of wood and mud plaster topped with thatched roofs of reeds or straw. If they had any windows, these were small openings covered with oiled paper.

Writing to future colonists from Plymouth in 1621, Edward Winslow advised them to "bring paper and linseed oil for your windows." Living conditions in New England soon improved, though. By 1629, Francis Higginson, another leader of the Massachusetts Bay Colony, was counseling emigrants to "be sure to furnish yourselves with glass for windows." After 1650 most homes in New England had hinged casement windows glazed with small square or diamond-shaped panes of glass.

The homes of well-to-do people in the southern colonies were built on an even grander scale, with larger windows. A traveler in Virginia in the late 1600s described them in these words: "Private homes have recently improved a great deal," he wrote, "many gentlemen here having built them in brick with many rooms on each floor, and several stories high. They always try to have large rooms which can be cool in summer. Lately they have made their rooms much loftier than they used to and the windows much larger and closed with glass."

The sash window, already popular in Holland and England, reached America about 1700. Because they were sturdier than the old casement windows, the wooden sashes could have a larger overall dimension and support bigger panes of glass, which glassmakers were now able to produce. As the size of the panes increased, the number of panes per window declined. A colonial window of 1730 might have had eighteen or twenty-four panes, but by the time the American Revolution began in 1776, most windows contained only twelve of the new, larger panes.

Curtains rarely appeared in all the windows of even the wealthiest colonial homes. They were made of heavy, expensive upholstery fabric and were often hung in only one room—the best bedchamber. When prosperous Americans had their portraits painted, they liked to be posed in front of a curtained sash window. It showed they were up-to-date people who possessed both wealth and taste.

Colonial window glass was quite costly because Great Britain required that it, like almost all manufactured goods, be imported from the mother country. Freight and tax

A girl in eighteenth-century America poses for her portrait in front of a sash window covered with a heavy, fringed drape. Painting by a folk artist known as the Beardsley limner.

charges were high, and the glass often arrived in a damaged condition from the long ocean voyage.

In Britain itself, windows were taxed starting in 1697 to help pay for the activities of the central government. The tax was first imposed on all houses with more than six windows, and it was increased several times during the 1700s. To save homeowners money while retaining a balanced pattern on the fronts and backs of their houses, architects included false windows in the walls. These were usually painted black and white in an attempt to make them look like actual window frames with glass in them.

America finally began to develop its own glassmaking industry in 1739, when a German immigrant named Casper Wistar defied the British ban on manufacturing and opened a glass factory in southern New Jersey. Wistar brought over skilled craftsmen from his native Germany to staff the factory and produced high-quality bottles, drinking vessels, and window glass. Benjamin Franklin was one of his early customers.

After the Revolutionary War ended with Britain's defeat in 1783, one glass factory after another opened in America. Now almost all the inhabitants of the original thirteen colonies could afford to have glass in their windows. But many people on the western frontier, which was then centered

Making window glass in an early nineteenth-century glass factory.

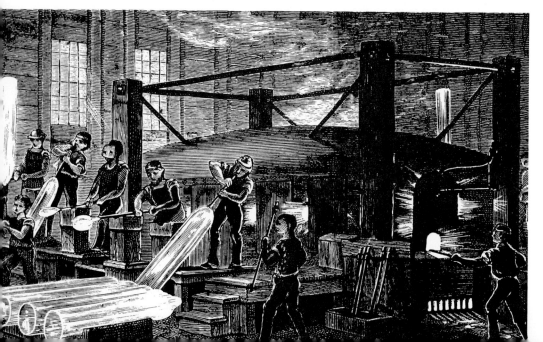

in Michigan, Ohio, and Kentucky, still had to make do with oiled paper. It was too difficult to ship glass overland on the rough, narrow roads of the time.

Most settlers on the frontier lived at first in log cabins. Such cabins were not an American invention, as many think, but were built originally in Scandinavia, where forests were thick and wood abundant. Immigrants from Sweden brought the idea of the log cabin with them when they settled in Delaware in 1638, and from there it traveled westward with the frontier.

Some log cabins had no windows at all when first built. A settler in Kentucky told a visitor in 1827: "We never make the windows in the first instance, but build up the walls with logs and then cut out the windows. Now I have not enough money to go into that matter, but I hope in the course of a year or so to put in a couple of glazed windows."

In early cabins the windows were usually small, no more than two logs in height. The pioneers cut them out carefully with drills and saws, and fitted boards to the ends of the logs with nails or pegs to make frames. Because their oiled-paper coverings were fragile, most log-cabin windows also had wooden shutters that could be closed as protection against wind, rain, and snow.

As living conditions on the frontier improved and people became more affluent, they often added onto their old log cabins. They enlarged the existing window openings, cut additional ones into the walls, and glazed all of them with glass.

To meet the growing demand for window glass on the frontier, the glass industry itself moved west. Pittsburgh

A Mormon family in frontier Utah gathers in front of their log cabin, which boasts a large, new glass window. Photo by A.J. Russell.

became a major glassmaking center in the early 1800s. Nearby coal deposits provided ample fuel, and convenient transportation along the Ohio River, and thence to the Mississippi, guaranteed a large market for the glass.

At the same time, dramatic advances were occurring in the glassmaking process. In 1832 the Chance brothers of Birmingham, England, invented machine-rolled glass. Now instead of each sheet being made laboriously by hand, the molten glass could be squeezed between rollers onto a flat iron plate. No longer did windowpanes have to be small. The new rolling process produced sheets of sturdy plate glass that measured as much as 2 feet by 4 feet.

Even though this new process made possible the mass production of glass for the first time, the price of plate glass in England was extremely high at first. This was because it was subject to a special tax based on weight. But English lawmakers repealed the glass tax in 1845, and in 1851 they also abolished the 150-year-old tax on windows. Now the way was cleared for builders to include larger windows than ever before in English homes, factories, and public buildings.

One of the most dramatic examples of this new trend was an immense structure that was built in London in 1851 to house the Great Exhibition of the Industry of All Nations. Queen Victoria's husband, Prince Albert, helped to organize the Exhibition, which was planned as a world's fair—the first ever held. On display would be the latest machinery and manufactured products from 15,000 exhibitors in nearly ninety countries.

Less than a year before the fair was scheduled to open in London's Hyde Park, Prince Albert and his royal commissioners invited the public to submit designs for the exhibition building. The design had to meet several conditions: No trees in the park were to be damaged or moved in order to make room for the building, which would have to be erected quickly and then dismantled just as quickly at the close of the exhibition.

Albert and the commissioners rejected more than 250 designs for brick and stone structures. Then Joseph Paxton, head gardener to the Duke of Devonshire, submitted a plan that met all their requirements. It called for a glass-and-iron building constructed of interchangeable, mass-produced sections that could be assembled easily.

Paxton's design was published in *The Illustrated London News* in July 1850 and won an enthusiastic response from the public. They nicknamed the building "The Crystal Palace" because it was so grand and contained so much glass.

Some builders resented the fact that Paxton, who was not a trained architect, had gotten such an important commission. But starting as a gardener's apprentice at the age of fifteen, Paxton had acquired a great deal of construction experience from designing greenhouses and conservatories.

In the early 1800s no English country house was thought to be complete unless it possessed a conservatory, or "orangery." The structure was called an orangery because orange trees often grew in it along with other exotic plants. Sometimes the orangery was separate from the main house and looked like a greenhouse; sometimes it was attached directly to the house. All orangeries had large windows in their walls; in fact, many orangery walls were composed entirely of windows.

By the mid-1800s, when plate glass was readily available

Exterior view of London's Crystal Palace.
COURTESY OF THE LIBRARY OF CONGRESS, PRINTS AND PHOTOGRAPHS DIVISION.

and the tax on it had been removed, some orangeries took on truly spectacular dimensions. The one Joseph Paxton designed for Chatsworth, the country estate of the Duke of Devonshire, was 277 feet long and 123 feet wide, and its arched glass roof rose to a height of 67 feet. The enclosure covered three quarters of an acre and was heated by eight boilers located in the basement. Tropical birds flew among the branches of palm trees planted in the orangery, and rare goldfish swam in its pools. The center aisle was wide enough for visitors to ride through in an open coach drawn by a pair of horses.

Paxton's success in designing orangeries such as this gave him the confidence to embark on his building for the Great Exhibition. He needed all the confidence he could get, for nothing like The Crystal Palace had ever been attempted before.

Paxton planned the building in the form of a cross, like a cathedral, with a nave crossed by a transept. But no cathedral was ever as big as The Crystal Palace. The nave extended to a length of 1,848 feet—over a third of a mile— and was flanked by side aisles with galleries above. Topping the structure, and rising to a height of 108 feet above the floor, was a roof of glass and iron.

A huge fountain marked the intersection of the transept and the nave. The transept itself was 408 feet long and had a curved roof made of glass and iron like the rest of the building. The curve was necessary in order to accommodate two tall elm trees that stood in the middle of the transept.

Work began on The Crystal Palace in August 1850, and had to be finished by the spring of 1851. To fulfill this almost impossible schedule, Paxton and his construction crew worked literally day and night. Iron foundries delivered over 2000 girders and 3000 columns to support the structure. The cast-iron frames for the walls and roof arrived in prefabricated sections. Paxton and his men glazed them with 300,000 panes of glass—the largest amount of glass used in any building up to that time.

To save time and effort, Paxton thought of an ingenious way to fit the panes into the roof. A group of four, two glaziers and two boys to mix their putty, worked from a special trolley whose wheels ran along the gutters. The group installed all the panes in one section, then pushed themselves along the roof to the next. In less than two weeks, the entire roof was glazed.

Thanks to such efficient methods, The Crystal Palace was completed on time. On May 1, 1851, Queen Victoria herself presided over the opening ceremony, which was attended by hundreds of prominent English men and women. They admired the impressive displays, but they marveled even more at the huge glass-and-iron building that housed them. So did the queen. In recognition of his accomplishment in designing and building The Crystal Palace, she knighted Joseph Paxton.

During the next six months, more than 6,000,000 people from all over the world visited the Great Exhibition and gazed in wonder at the transparent walls and roof of The Crystal Palace. Londoners liked the building so much that they refused to allow it to be destroyed after the Exhibition closed in October 1851. They arranged to have it moved to Sydenham, a southern suburb of London, and Joseph

Queen Victoria officially opens the Great Exhibition in The Crystal Palace on May 1, 1851.

Paxton enlarged the structure and designed a park to surround it. The Palace reopened in 1854 and remained a popular tourist attraction and entertainment center until it was destroyed by fire in 1936.

Meanwhile, The Crystal Palace had a far-reaching effect on exhibition buildings elsewhere. In 1853 New York City held its own international exhibition of art and manufactured goods in a structure with glass walls that looked much like those in The Crystal Palace. However, there were several important differences. To avoid undue glare, translucent rather than clear glass was used in the 15,000 panes of the New York Crystal Palace. And the roof and dome over the New York building were covered with wood and tin instead

The New York Crystal Palace.

of glass. The builders feared that heavy snowfalls, which were common in New York in winter, would do too much damage to a glass roof.

Glass-walled buildings like the Crystal Palaces in London and New York also had a tremendous influence on late-nineteenth-century architecture. People liked the openness and lightness of such structures and saw ways to utilize their features in other types of buildings.

Architects in New York and other cities developed cast-iron building fronts that were shaped to resemble stone or marble columns and usually painted gray. But unlike stone, these cast-iron fronts were thin and lightweight, and they contained large windows made of single sheets of plate glass. The ground-floor windows in the buildings gave merchants the opportunity to create attractive displays of the goods offered for sale in their shops. The windows on the upper floors admitted far more light and air into the offices than the small, twelve-paned windows of earlier business blocks.

Not everyone admired the new iron-and-glass buildings.

Under the central dome of the New York Crystal Palace.

John Ruskin, the noted critic, conceded that The Crystal Palace and structures like it were marvelous feats of engineering, but he said they certainly weren't works of art. Other critics expressed even more negative views. One called iron-and-glass exhibition halls and railroad terminals "mere sheds."

In reaction to the mass-production techniques that Joseph Paxton and other builders were employing, an alternative approach emerged. In England it was known as the Arts and Crafts Movement, in America it was called the Aesthetic Movement. Its followers emphasized the virtues of Gothic architecture with its arches and decorative stonework. And they urged people to once again include stained-glass windows in their churches, public buildings, and homes.

NINE

❖

The Return of the Stained-Glass Window

The 1870s ushered in a period of great prosperity in both England and the United States. Ruled by Queen Victoria, the British Empire extended across all seven continents of the globe. The United States put aside memories of its bloody Civil War and expanded westward at a rapid rate.

Along with prosperity came a renewed interest in religion. Queen Victoria herself set the tone for this religious revival by putting great emphasis on traditional moral values in her speeches and actions. The British and American people responded by building thousands of churches, most of them in the popular Gothic style. More than 4000 churches of different denominations were under construction in the U.S. in the single year of 1888. And all but the poorest of these included at least one stained-glass window. For the first time in years, stained-glass makers in Europe and America had more work than they could handle.

Many of the windows were made of brilliant pot-metal glass, like the church windows of the Middle Ages. Prominent English artists such as William Morris and Edward Burne-Jones created hundreds of striking designs for church windows. The designs often featured single central figures against backgrounds of vines, plants, fruits, and flowers.

Well-to-do people who attended church regularly saw the light streaming through the beautiful stained-glass windows and began to want similar windows in the grand, new mansions they were building for themselves. They installed stained-glass windows in hallways, on stair landings, and in bathrooms, and inserted panels of stained glass above panes of clear glass in living- and dining-room windows. A stained-glass panel above the front door often incorporated the street number of the house.

For those who couldn't afford stained glass in their windows, there was a cheaper alternative. They could buy decorative patterns and borders printed on colored paper, cut them out, and stick them on their clear windows with a thin glue. Although the patterns tended to wear out quickly from the effects of heat and cold, they provided a colorful effect when they were new and fresh. Homemaking magazines of the time praised them, and said that gluing the patterns on windows was "a pleasant occupation for ladies and gentlemen alike."

In the 1880s stained-glass windows also appeared in the city halls that were built at the time, in department stores, and in the first-class sleeping cars on the new transcontinental railroads that crisscrossed the U.S. They could even be found on steamboats. In his book *Life on the Mississippi*, Mark Twain described the windows on a boat: "Lovely rainbow-light fell everywhere from the colored glazing of the skylights; it made a soul-satisfying spectacle."

To meet the increased demand for stained-glass windows, several outstanding new designers appeared on the scene in the United States. The first of these was John La Farge.

The son of wealthy French immigrants, La Farge studied law for a time but gave it up in 1858 to become the artist he had always wanted to be. After establishing himself as a skillful painter of landscapes and still lifes, he turned his attention in the 1870s to designs for stained-glass windows.

La Farge is credited with what many think was the greatest contribution to stained-glass making since the Middle Ages: the invention of opalescent, or multi-colored, glass. Like many other inventions, it was inspired by an accident. One day La Farge took a long look at a tooth powder jar that had been carelessly made of milky glass that was streaked with different colors. He realized that by using such opalescent glass in his windows, he could create unusual effects of color and texture. (*See color insert.*)

In some of his early windows La Farge included glass cut right out of bottles and jars to serve as visual accents. The surfaces of many of his windows were not flat. For example, the West Window that he designed for Boston's Trinity Church contained globes of turquoise glass the size of golf balls mixed together with red and green glass from wine bottles.

In other windows, La Farge used specially manufactured glasses that were streaked like the glass in the tooth powder jar, textured with rollers, or deliberately cracked and fractured. Sometimes he even combined glass with amethysts and other semiprecious stones to create jewellike effects in his designs.

La Farge was a great admirer of Japanese paintings and prints, which had been seen widely in Europe and America since Commodore Perry's historic visit to Japan in 1854 and the opening of trade between Japan and the West that followed. With the new materials and methods for stained-glass making that he had developed, La Farge was able to simulate in his windows many of the favorite subjects of Japanese art. He duplicated the velvety texture of peony blossoms, the play of light on a goldfish's scales, and the multicolored feathers in a peacock's tail.

Another American designer of stained glass made his debut in the late 1870s, and soon his reputation outshone John La Farge's. This designer's name was Louis Comfort Tiffany.

Tiffany was the son of the founder of the famous New York silver and jewelry store that still bears the family name. As a boy Louis liked to collect the colored pebbles and bits of broken glass that he picked up on the beach in front of his family's summer home at Montauk, Long Island. In 1866, when he was eighteen, Louis announced that he wished to study art rather than go to college or enter the family business. He took lessons from the well-known painter George Inness and discovered that he had a flair for landscape painting.

During the winter of 1868–69, Tiffany visited the major art centers of Europe. He was especially impressed by the twelfth- and thirteenth-century stained-glass windows he saw in Chartres Cathedral. Returning to America, Tiffany continued to paint, but he devoted more and more of his time to interior decoration. "I am going into decorative work as a profession," he wrote to a friend, "because I see it as a way to provide good art to American homes." He also became interested in the possibilities of stained glass, and in 1878 designed his first stained-glass window.

Tiffany believed that a designer should be responsible for his windows from beginning to end; that included everything from overseeing the manufacture of the glass to directing the glazier in its cutting and arrangement. Like John La Farge, with whom he worked for a time, Tiffany used a great deal of opalescent glass in his designs. Many of his windows also achieved a three-dimensional effect. A critic made note of this in describing a Tiffany window that pictured round, purple eggplants: "When the sunlight streams in through such a window, it is as if the real object, rendered transparent in all its tissues, filled the space."

In his later career Tiffany supervised the entire decoration of many great houses, designing everything from lamps to floor and wall coverings to draperies, furniture, and, of course, windows. The last house that Tiffany designed was one for himself, Laurelton Hall in Oyster Bay, New York, completed in 1904. It contained many beautiful stained-glass windows, including several that featured hanging clusters of luscious purple grapes, rendered in three-dimensional opalescent glass. (*See color insert.*)

A third designer of stained-glass windows was one of America's and the world's greatest modern architects: Frank Lloyd Wright. Born in Richland, Wisconsin, Wright studied civil engineering at the University of Wisconsin, then worked for seven years in a Chicago architectural firm. After deciding to strike out on his own in 1893, Wright established himself in Oak Park, a suburb of Chicago, and built a series of residences for well-to-do clients.

Instead of designing the houses in the popular Gothic style, with its high ceilings and elaborate decorations, Wright pioneered a new, simpler style. Like Tiffany and La Farge,

Frederick C. Robie house, Chicago, Illinois, one of the "prairie houses" designed by Frank Lloyd Wright. Photograph by Cervin Robinson from the Historic American Buildings Survey.

Wright was a great admirer of Japanese art and architecture. He was especially impressed with the way Japanese architects united the inside rooms of a house with the garden outside. He tried to achieve a similar effect in the houses he built in Oak Park by employing low, horizontal lines, overhanging eaves, and continuous bands of windows. Because the homes related so closely to the flat landscape surrounding them, people began calling them Wright's "prairie houses."

Most of the windows in the prairie houses were glazed with clear glass that afforded broad views of the lawns and gardens. But Wright filled some with stained glass for color and contrast. There were no peonies, grapes, or peacocks in Wright's window designs. In their place he developed patterns that were as new and unique as the prairie houses themselves.

Wright appreciated the realistic scenes that were pictured in medieval church windows but felt that approach was unsuitable for modern windows. "Nothing is more annoying to me than any tendency toward realism of form in window glass," he said. "Stained-glass windows today should be shimmering fabrics, woven in rich glass. They should be things of delicate beauty consistent with slender steel construction and expressing the nature of that construction."

Wright believed that houses were like living organisms, and that every part should relate to every other part. His designs for stained-glass windows reflected this belief. He often started by sketching an actual flower or plant, and then broke it down into basic abstract shapes until he arrived at a pleasing geometrical composition. "I try to capture

A pair of stained- and clear-glass windows, designed by Frank Lloyd Wright for the Robie House. Photograph by Cervin Robinson for the Historic American Buildings Survey.

the essence of the plant in my designs," Wright said.

Because Wright's windows contained exact circles, squares, rectangles, and triangles, each piece of glass in them required extremely precise cutting and fitting. Wright himself would often go to the Chicago glassmaking studio and sit down with the manager to lay out a window. They selected the pieces for the design from bins of beautifully colored glass and laid them out on the pattern Wright had drawn, just as stained-glass makers had done in the Middle Ages.

Wright's most lively and colorful window designs were probably those he created in 1912 for the playhouse in the Avery Coonley residence in Riverside, Illinois. The playhouse wasn't intended for the Coonleys' own children but for a kindergarten that Mrs. Coonley owned and operated.

The tall windows in the playhouse featured circles of red, blue, and green glass that looked like balloons for a child's birthday party. The designs resembled some of the abstract paintings that European artists were doing at the time, and the later geometric paintings of the Dutch artist Piet Mondrian. But Wright's windows were not paintings. Like all the elements in his houses, they performed a useful function, bringing light and cheer into the kindergarten where Mrs. Coonley's pupils played and studied. (See color insert.)

Wright continued to use stained glass in the windows of houses he designed until 1923, when he gave it up in favor of clear plate glass. By then stained glass had gone out of fashion, along with the other elaborate decorations of the Gothic Revival style. Architects looked instead to Joseph Paxton's Crystal Palace for inspiration and began to design office buildings, apartment houses, and homes that emphasized the clean, simple lines of their steel-frame construction. These buildings demanded large window areas; in fact, some of the new buildings seemed to be composed of nothing but windows!

TEN

❖

Glass Towers and Bombs

In the closing years of the nineteenth century, Chicago led the way in the construction of tall, large-windowed office buildings. There were several reasons for this boom. Located between New York and San Francisco, Chicago was one of America's busiest centers of railroading and commerce. And many of the old buildings in the heart of the city had been destroyed in the Great Fire of 1871.

Chicago was the home of the first steel-framed sky-scraper, the ten-story Home Insurance Company Building erected in 1884. During the next twenty years one sky-scraper after another rose in the bustling Loop district near the shore of Lake Michigan. The most original and modern of these—especially in the way its windows were treated—

was the fourteen-story Reliance Building, designed by Daniel Burnham and John Wellborn Root and completed in 1894.

The Reliance Building featured what were known as "Chicago windows," since the style first appeared in the new skyscrapers. A Chicago window had three sections— a single large pane of glass in the middle and a narrow sash at either end that could be opened and closed.

Most Chicago windows were set in bays, with the movable

The Reliance Building in Chicago.
COURTESY OF THE LIBRARY OF CONGRESS, PRINTS AND PHOTOGRAPHS DIVISION.

sashes at an angle so that when they were raised in the hot summer months, they would catch the slightest breeze. The bay windows in the Reliance Building were noteworthy because they were twice the usual size and covered almost the entire surface of the building.

Its glassy walls, like the ones in the Crystal Palaces, drew much attention to the Reliance Building when it was new. But unlike those temporary exhibition structures, the Reliance Building and its windows were not intended to create a passing sensation. Instead the windows were meant to bring as much light and air as possible into the floors of an office building. And they're still serving that purpose today, almost a hundred years later.

The ground floor of the Reliance Building, like the ground floors of most of the early skyscrapers, was filled with retail shops. They displayed their merchandise behind large plate-glass windows, as did the huge six- and seven-story department stores that were now common in all the major cities of America and Europe. Brightly lit by the new electric lights, the window displays in these stores attracted the attention of the crowds that flocked into downtown districts at night. As a magazine of the time said, "There has grown up a large class of 'window shoppers' who study the display windows after supper, comparing qualities and prices and making up their minds where to do their purchasing."

Along with office workers and window shoppers, factory workers also benefited from the new emphasis that was being put on large window areas in buildings. Two German architects, Walter Gropius and Adolf Meyer, pioneered the new style in factories with their plans for the Fagus Factory, built in 1911. The floors of the factory jutted out slightly from the supporting columns. This allowed the walls to be composed almost entirely of glass, and the glass panes of one side butted against the glass panes of another at the corners.

A German writer, Paul Scheerbart, expressed the feelings many people had about glass-walled buildings in an article he wrote in 1914. "If we wish to raise our culture to a

A corner of the Fagus Factory, designed by Walter Gropius and Adolf Meyer.
COURTESY OF THE MUSEUM OF MODERN ART, NEW YORK.

higher level, we are forced for better or worse to transform our architecture," Scheerbart said. "This will be possible only if we remove the enclosed quality from the spaces in which we live. This can be done through the introduction of glass architecture that lets the sunlight and the light of the moon and the stars into our rooms—not merely through a few windows, but simultaneously through the greatest number of walls that are made entirely of glass."

The first architect to make Scheerbart's vision a reality was not a German but an American, Willis Polk of San Francisco. Polk had trained in Chicago with Daniel Burnham, an architect of the Reliance Building. He admired Burnham's use of glass and carried his teacher's ideas a step further when he designed the Hallidie Building in San Franciso in 1917.

Polk didn't fill the spaces between columns with glass, as Burnham and other earlier architects had done. Instead he hung the glass front of the structure on brackets that projected out a foot from the reinforced-concrete floors. The result was the first building in the world to have a facade, or curtain wall, composed entirely of glass.

When the Hallidie Building was first opened, it created quite a stir. Some nicknamed it "The Daylight Building"; others called it "The Frontless Building." People wondered what would happen to it if another earthquake struck San Francisco. But the people who worked in it loved its light-filled offices. And the building's glass facade remains in place today, undamaged by the tremors that have occasionally shaken it over the years.

World War I ended in 1918, a year after the Hallidie

Making plate glass in an early-twentieth-century glass factory.

Building was completed. Architects in Europe and America rejoiced along with everyone else, and looked forward hopefully to a time of peace, prosperity, and new construction. They wanted to express the dynamic qualities of modern life in their designs and relied on steel and glass to help them achieve their goals.

Fortunately, steel was now being mass-produced, window glass was cheaper than ever and came in all shapes and sizes, and developments in insulation lessened the need for thick walls and roofs to keep out the heat and cold. The way was now open for glass-walled structures in the style of the Hallidie Building, and architects responded with exciting new plans.

Ludwig Mies van der Rohe's 1920 drawing for a triangular glass-and-steel skyscraper. From The Mies van der Rohe Archive.

In 1920 a young German architect, Ludwig Mies van der Rohe, entered a design competition for an office building in Berlin. After trying several different approaches, he submitted a drawing for a twenty-story skyscraper of glass and steel the likes of which had never been seen before.

The glass walls of the triangular building rose uninterrupted to the top, where they simply stopped as though cut off by a pair of shears. Nothing was solid in the structure except the steel skeleton—the "bones," as Mies called it—which was set back inside the glass "skin," and the core of elevators at the center of the building. Mies meant this skin-and-bones construction to leave the interior space on each floor completely open and unobstructed. The occupants could divide and subdivide it in any way they wanted; only the exterior walls of glass—the great windows—would always be there.

The judges of the competition rejected Mies' design on the ground that it was unsuitable for the site, but this didn't stop the determined young architect. He went on in 1922 to design another skyscraper project, this one for a thirty-two-story building with curving glass walls. According to Mies, he got the idea for its form after studying the play of light on a small model that he hung outside his office window.

In 1922 Mies also designed a very different kind of office building. It had only seven stories, and the walls were not all glass like those in his skyscrapers. Instead, each of the reinforced-concrete floor slabs turned up at the ends to form a wall, and these walls were topped with bands of windows. Mies called them "ribbon windows" because they ran in a continuous line around the building.

The seven-story office building, like Mies' two skyscrapers, never got beyond the drawing stage. But Mies employed ribbon windows in an apartment house that was actually erected in Stuttgart, Germany, in 1927. He also used large window areas in the Tugendhat house that he built in Brno, Czechoslovakia, in 1930.

Mies' drawing for a concrete office building with ribbon windows. From The Mies van der Rohe Archive.

Mies agreed with Frank Lloyd Wright that a house should be more than "a box with holes punched in it," an expression Wright had once used. For the Tugendhat house, Mies designed two outer walls of glass that commanded views of the garden and the city beyond. At the press of a button, sections of the walls slid automatically into the floor, thereby uniting the living room with the garden outside. This created a feeling of openness similar to the effect achieved by the sliding paper panels in Japanese houses.

Other architects took up Mies' ideas for windows and incorporated them in their own designs. George Howe and William Lescaze used ribbon windows on the narrow ends of the thirty-two-story Philadelphia Savings Fund Society Building, completed in 1932, and carried the idea of a glass skin further by bending the windows around the building's corners.

Erich Mendelsohn employed windows in an even more dramatic way in the Schocken Department Store, which was erected in the German city of Chemnitz in 1930. He gave the building a sleek, curved shape and encircled it with bands of large ribbon windows. When they were lit at night, the windows made the store look like a glittering modern fairyland.

The lights in the Schocken store and thousands of other buildings in Europe didn't remain shining for long, however. Their windows and glass facades were soon to be threatened by one of the most devastating periods in twentieth-century history: World War II.

Even before actual fighting broke out in September 1939, there were hints of what was to come. Architects such as Mies van der Rohe, whose modernist ideas clashed with those held by the Nazis, and Erich Mendelsohn, who was Jewish, were forced to flee Germany. And the events of

The Schocken Department Store, designed by Erich Mendelsohn.
COURTESY OF THE MUSEUM OF MODERN ART, NEW YORK.

Kristallnacht in November 1938 proved to be a ghastly pre-view of the war's destruction.

The background to *Kristallnacht* was complicated. In the fall of 1938 Nazi Germany ordered all foreign-born Jews to leave the country, including the parents of seventeen-year-old Hershl Grynszpan, who was away at school in Paris. Although the Grynszpans were Polish citizens, they had lived in Germany since 1914, and Poland refused to allow them to reenter the country. Instead they and hundreds of other Poles who had been expelled were forced to stay in a detention camp on the Polish-German border.

When young Hershl heard what had happened to his parents, he lost control of himself. Taking a handgun, he went to the German embassy in Paris on November 7, 1938, and shot the first person he met, a minor official named Ernst von Rath. The Nazis played up the incident in the German press, calling it a typical example of Jewish treachery. And when von Rath died of his wounds two days later, it gave the Nazis an excuse to launch a huge new crackdown on the Jews in Germany.

On the night of November 10, with the encouragement of Adolf Hitler, Joseph Goebbels, and other German leaders, members of the Nazi party and the dreaded S.S. attacked Jewish synagogues and stores throughout Germany and Austria. The mobs smashed one store window after another and threw rocks through the priceless stained-glass windows in many of Germany's largest synagogues.

So much broken glass littered the streets that it gave the night the name by which it has been known ever since— *Kristallnacht*, Night of Broken Glass. It was later estimated

A German store window smashed during Kristallnacht.

that the amount of plate glass shattered that night equaled half the annual production of Belgium, from which most of the glass had been imported.

Over 700 Jewish stores were wrecked during *Kristallnacht*, 76 synagogues were destroyed, and 191 others were damaged. Nearly a hundred Jews were killed, and thousands of others were arrested when they tried to defend themselves and their businesses. But the Nazis made no apologies. Instead, when insurance payments for the damage done on *Kristallnacht* were made to Jews, the Nazis arranged to confiscate the money. And the Jews were still made liable for repairing the damage—including all the cracked and broken windows.

Kristallnacht was only the beginning. After the Nazis launched World War II less than a year later, their bombers inflicted far greater damage on cities and towns all across western Europe and Great Britain. London and other British cities tried to gird for air attacks by crisscrossing windows with tape, and by blacking them out at night with heavy curtains and blinds. But these measures did little good when the Nazis began their all-out *blitzkrieg* attack on Great Britain in September 1940. *Blitzkrieg* means "lightning war," but the British shortened it to "the Blitz."

Day after day squadrons of German bombers pounded London in an attempt to force the British to surrender, as France had done the previous June. At first they aimed their deadly loads at industrial targets, but soon they started hitting residential and government districts in the British capital also.

One afternoon in late September, Neville Chamberlain, the former Prime Minister and still a government leader, was presiding over a meeting when the bombers arrived. Behind Chamberlain was a large bay window, and his private secretary urged him to move away from it. Chamberlain thanked the secretary for his concern but stayed where he was.

As bombs began to explode nearby, the secretary became agitated and suggested they all adjourn to a shelter in the basement. No, said Chamberlain, not unless the others wished to do so.

A moment later a bomb in the next block shook the panes in the bay window. Wanting to protect Chamberlain from the danger of flying glass, the secretary jumped up and started to draw the drapes.

Chamberlain stopped him by saying, "Let's have the day-light while it's there." And the meeting went on.

Most British people stood up to the bombings as bravely as Chamberlain, and by mid-October the Nazis had virtually

ceased their daylight raids. By then British fighters and anti-aircraft fire had brought down over a thousand German planes.

The Germans switched now to nighttime raids and focused on industrial targets in such cities as Liverpool,

COURTESY OF THE LIBRARY OF CONGRESS, PRINTS AND PHOTOGRAPHS DIVISION.

Above: *London firemen fight a blaze in the aftermath of a Nazi air raid. All the windows in the nearby buildings have been shattered by exploding bombs.*

Left: *Buildings hit during a Nazi air raid tumble into London street. Behind them can be seen the dome of St. Paul's Cathedral.*

COURTESY OF THE LIBRARY OF CONGRESS, PRINTS AND PHOTOGRAPHS DIVISION.

Manchester, Birmingham, and Coventry. On November 14, a clear, moonless night, they attempted a knockout blow on Coventry. Between four and five hundred bombers flew in relays over the city for eleven hours from dusk to dawn.

A hundred acres in the center of Coventry were devastated, nearly a thousand houses were totally demolished and another 32,000 were damaged. Broken glass from shattered windows was everywhere. The famed Coventry Cathedral, one of the oldest and most beautiful in England, caught fire, and by morning only its fifteenth-century spire and a few ruined walls remained standing. All its historic stained-glass windows had been destroyed.

Even though 554 people in Coventry were killed during the raid, it didn't stop the city. Within twenty-four hours the local government was functioning again, and within two months production in the city's factories was back to normal. In Coventry—as in other English cities—the Nazi Blitz had failed to achieve its goal.

Later in the war many German cities suffered greater damage than London and Coventry. British and American bombers pounded Berlin night after night, and on February 13–14, 1945, when the war was nearing its end, they struck Dresden. The bombers missed the industrial targets they were aiming for and hit instead the cultural heart of the old medieval city. The castle, the opera house, the state theater, the cathedral, and five other churches with centuries-old stained-glass windows went up in flames. Thousands of citizens lost their homes and all their possessions. More than 35,000 people were killed.

The greatest damage of all, though, was inflicted on Ger-

The bombed-out shell of Coventry Cathedral in England has been preserved as a memorial.

many's partner in the war, Japan. Firebombing raids on Tokyo reduced entire districts of wood-and-paper houses to ashes. And the atomic bombs that fell on Hiroshima and Nagasaki in August 1945 created unimaginable scenes of destruction.

Near the center of each of the two blasts, people were blown against the walls of their dwellings or offices by the force of the explosion, or were crushed to death under collapsed houses. Many were injured by glass splinters and other flying debris even at distances far from the center.

In Hiroshima all buildings within a mile and a half of the blast were totally demolished, and 92 percent of the city's buildings were damaged to some extent. The blast shattered windows as far away as twenty-two miles to the southwest.

In Nagasaki the completely demolished area extended up to two miles from the center of the explosion. Partial destruction occurred for an additional two miles, and broken windows could be found more than fifteen miles beyond that radius.

About 350,000 people were living in Hiroshima at the time the atomic bomb hit, and there were approximately 270,000 in Nagasaki. At least 65,000 civilians died as a result of the blast and its immediate aftermath in Hiroshima, 39,000 in Nagasaki. But many bodies were never found, and it has been estimated that as many as 150,000 people may actually have been killed in Hiroshima and 75,000 in Nagasaki.

Even before the war finally ended in that August of 1945, people in Europe and Asia had begun to make plans to rebuild their homes and cities. A new, international style of glass-and-steel architecture came into being to meet their needs. And after all the years of blackouts and broken glass, it included more and bigger windows than ever.

ELEVEN

❖

A House Made of Windows

Construction of commercial buildings boomed in all the major American cities after World War II ended in 1945. There was a pent-up need for office space because few new buildings had been built during the war years and the twelve years of economic depression that preceded them.

New skyscrapers also rose from the ruins of London, Berlin, Moscow, Tokyo, and other cities that had been hard hit by the war. Most of them were designed in the glass-and-steel "International Style" that had been pioneered in the 1920s and 1930s by Walter Gropius, Le Corbusier, Ludwig Mies van der Rohe, and other architects. This style employed structural materials that were used in their natural form instead of being covered with decoration; wood was wood, brick was brick, steel was steel. It also used a great

123

deal of glass to welcome in the sun and provide office workers with far-reaching views.

The development of tinted glass helped make the new glass-walled buildings possible. The metallic oxides that gave tinted glass its gray, blue-green, or bronze color admitted light while reducing solar brightness and glare. The oxides in the glass also absorbed up to 35 percent of the sun's heat. They reradiated it back into the atmosphere, thereby lowering the demands on a building's air-conditioning equipment.

The first important building to use tinted glass in its windows was Lever House, designed by Gordon Bunshaft and erected in New York City in 1952. Viewed from the street, Lever House is a twenty-one-story slab of blue-green glass and stainless steel resting atop a low, horizontal slab of the same materials. Because glass panels instead of brick or stone were used to cover the wall sections between the floors, Lever House presents an all-glass appearance.

To keep its glass surface clean, the building's owners developed a unique type of window-washing equipment that served as a model for later glass skyscrapers. The equipment came in two parts. The first part, a 10.5-ton power plant and crane, ran on standard railroad tracks around the rim of the building's roof. The second part, called the gondola, moved up and down the sides of the building on stainless-steel tracks set six windows apart. The gondola was attached to the vertical tracks by grippers that prevented tilting and tipping. Cables extending down from the arms of the rooftop crane helped to keep the gondola from swaying.

COURTESY OF LEVER BROTHERS COMPANY.

A two-man window-washing crew descends the side of the Lever House in a gondola, suspended from a crane on the roof.

A two-man crew in the gondola controlled its up-and-down movement by push buttons, washing the six-window section from top to bottom. Then they returned to the top, where they pushed another button to move the crane and its power plant horizontally to the next six-window strip. There the gondola's grippers automatically found the vertical tracks, and the crew was ready for another window-washing trip down the walls of the building. It took the two men six working days to clean the entire surface of Lever House, including its 1,404 windows.

Other new glass skyscrapers competed with Lever House for attention in New York and other cities. Several of the most striking were designed by Mies van der Rohe, who finally got a chance to build the kind of all-glass structure he had first dreamed of in the 1920s.

Mies' high-rise Lake Shore Drive apartments opened in Chicago in 1951. The two twenty-six-story towers of black steel and glass were set at right angles to each other and were connected by a steel canopy. Many of the apartments had spectacular views of Lake Michigan from their floor-to-ceiling windows set in aluminum frames. In order to present a uniform appearance from the outside, all the window draperies used in the apartments had to be the same pale gray. But Mies provided an inner curtain track for those who preferred another color inside their rooms.

The *Chicago Tribune* described the Lake Shore Drive apartments in an article entitled "People *Do* Live in Glass Houses." The article wondered about the psychological effect of living "high in the air with no solid walls to mark off one's quarters from the abyss outside." People seemed to enjoy the experience, for Mies' apartments were soon filled. They have remained popular in the years since, as have similar glass-walled apartment towers that sprang up later in cities all across America.

Mies went on to design another pace-setting glass tower, the Seagram Building, which was erected in New York City in 1958. Located across Park Avenue from Lever House, the thirty-eight-story Seagram Building rises from a plaza

The twin towers of the Lake Shore Drive apartments in Chicago, designed by Ludwig Mies van der Rohe.

that makes it appear to be even taller. Its floor-to-ceiling windows of pinkish-gray glass are divided by bronze mullions that sweep from the bottom of the building to the top.

Around the perimeter of each of the thirty-eight floors is a band of lighted ceiling panels. In the daytime these panels effectively minimize the contrast in brightness between the office interiors and the sky. At night, lighted on all floors at one fifth the daytime intensity, they give the building a warm glow through its tinted windows.

The bronze-and-glass slab of Mies' Seagram Building rises at the left on Park Avenue in New York City. To the right can be seen the edge of Lever House.

From the time it was completed, people stood in awe of the Seagram Building. Countless architects imitated it more or less successfully, and it helped to set a pattern for glass-and-steel office buildings everywhere.

The postwar years also saw new developments in residential windows. As the United States became more populous and affluent, more and more people moved to suburbs

A picture window in a postwar suburban home.

surrounding the major cities. Because of land, labor, and building costs, the one-story ranch house often replaced the two-story structures of earlier housing booms. Instead of houses with many rooms and small windows, builders of the new ranch-style houses frequently combined two rooms into one and included a large, three-part Chicago window in it. Thus the picture window was born.

Like the windows in Frank Lloyd Wright's prairie houses,

picture windows flooded the rooms with light and helped to abolish the barrier between the outdoors and the interior. To reduce heat loss in winter, many of the windows also functioned as insulating units. They were formed of two pieces of glass with a dry air space between them. Often called "twindows," these insulated windows were soon being made of tinted glass as well as clear. Now architects had a window that could do two jobs: Besides helping to keep the house warm in winter, it controlled solar heat gain and glare in summer.

With the aid of insulated glass, people began to install even larger windows in their homes. Sliding glass doors and large "window wall" panels like those Mies van der Rohe had used in the Tugendhat house in 1930 became common features in many suburban homes. Finally architect Philip Johnson went all the way and designed a house for himself that was composed entirely of windows.

Located in New Canaan, Connecticut, and completed in 1949, the Glass House is surrounded by woods and overlooks a pond. Eight black, H-shaped steel columns form the house's structural framework, with large sheets of clear glass fitted between them. The only solid element in the house is a brick cylinder in the middle that contains a fireplace and the bathroom.

When the Glass House was first completed, people drove from miles around to stare at it, creating traffic jams on the nearby roads. The famous architect Frank Lloyd Wright, then an old man, came to see it and said to Philip Johnson: "Philip, should I take my hat off or leave it on? Am I indoors

Philip Johnson's Glass House in New Canaan, Connecticut.

or out?" Some critics likened the house to "living in a fishbowl."

But Johnson defended his unusual design. "I was brought up on a sleeping porch, so I'm used to this," he said. "I don't believe in indoor-outdoor space; here the natural environment serves as expensive wallpaper. It's like living in the weather."

Few people followed Johnson's lead and built glass houses for themselves, however. By the 1960s, new threats to windows of all kinds had emerged. From stained-glass windows in churches to display windows in big-city stores to picture windows in suburban homes and schools, the very idea of the window seemed to be in danger.

TWELVE

❖

New Threats to Windows

After World War II ended, church officials in Europe brought their precious stained-glass windows out of storage and reinstalled them in windows that had been boarded over during the conflict. Prominent modern artists such as Henri Matisse and Fernand Léger designed stained-glass windows for new chapels and churches. Marc Chagall created his beautiful "Twelve Tribes of Israel" windows for the Hadassah Synagogue in Jerusalem. And Louis Tiffany's elaborate windows came back into style.

Just when interest in stained-glass windows was reaching a new height, they were menaced by a threat greater than any revolution or war. The enemy was air pollution. In Cologne, West Germany, air pollutants from the nearby railway station and the city's factories have corroded the exterior surface of the glass in the city's famed cathedral, reducing its thickness year by year.

In England stained-glass windows are exposed to heavy smog, and those in Canterbury Cathedral have suffered especially severe damage. Pits have formed in many of the cathedral's magnificent windows. Through them acid rain can reach the inner surface of the glass and eat into the paintwork there.

To combat this destruction, preservation experts in England, Germany, and other countries are beginning to double-glaze the stained-glass windows in their churches. A protective pane of glass, not attached to the stained-glass panel, is installed over it. The temperature and humidity between the pane and the panel can be controlled, thereby preventing corrosion of the stained glass by sulfur dioxide and other pollutants. With the aid of double glazing, preservationists hope to insure that the precious centuries-old windows will survive for hundreds of years to come.

A totally different threat to store, school, and home windows sprang up in the 1960s. Filled with anger, frustration, or boredom, thousands of Americans engaged in rioting and acts of vandalism that resulted in the destruction of vast numbers of windows of all kinds.

Teenage vandalism was particularly costly in the suburbs. Roving bands of youngsters aimed BB guns at picture windows in homes and threw rocks through school windows. To help prevent window breaking, schools in Milwaukee, Phoenix, and Kansas City, Missouri, began in the 1970s to install panes of tough plastic rather than glass in their windows. New schools were built with few or no exterior windows—only skylights, or windows facing on inner courtyards like the houses of ancient times.

Vandalism took a different form in America's inner cities. There, landlords frequently stopped maintaining apartment buildings that were no longer profitable, and drug addicts and derelicts moved in. Soon the windows in the buildings were broken, and fires often broke out, leaving the structures burned-out shells. At that point the city usually took over and either demolished what was left of the buildings or bricked in all the doors and windows to prevent further destruction. In New York City and other localities, officials sometimes hired artists to paint flowerpots and curtains on the bricked-up windows so they would present a cheerier picture to passersby.

The race riots that occurred in Detroit, Washington, Los Angeles, Newark, and many other places in the late 1960s took a heavy toll of inner-city store windows. Looting accompanied most of the riots, and it usually began with someone throwing a rock through the display window of an appliance, clothing, or liquor store. In the Detroit riot of 1967 looters broke into dozens of stores in a sixteen-block area within an hour of the time rioting started. At the height of the Newark riot, looting spread to ten of the city's twenty-three square miles. Property damage—mainly from window breaking, looting, and fires—was estimated at more than $15 million.

In Newark, as in other riot-torn cities, many businesses never reopened after they were looted. Some stores were completely destroyed in the riots; others were abandoned

Boarded-up store windows in Buffalo, New York, following nine hours of rioting in June 1967.

and then torn down years later. Waist-high grass and weeds often grow in vacant lots where the stores once stood, and the ground is still littered with broken glass from their windows.

If the stores did reopen, the owners usually walled in the display windows with cement blocks rather than risk having them broken again. As a result, many inner-city business blocks today look more like fortresses than shopping streets.

The energy crisis of the 1970s presented yet another threat to the windows in homes, schools, and office buildings. The all-glass architectural styles of the postwar years had depended on a steady supply of inexpensive fuel for heating and air-conditioning. Now there was a danger that that supply might be cut off, or drastically reduced.

To conserve energy and meet the demand for even better climate control in buildings, manufacturers developed an improved window covering—reflective glass. Reflective glass was coated with a thin, transparent metallic film. This mirrorlike coating reflected the sun's rays away from the glass and lowered heat gain within the building much more than mere tinted glass could. As a consequence, buildings sheathed in reflective glass required smaller, less powerful air-conditioning units.

Reflective glass covers the headquarters of R. J. Reynolds Industries in Winston-Salem, N.C.

COURTESY OF PPG INDUSTRIES, INC.

Reflective glass also changed the look of the factories and office buildings that were covered with it. Many people enjoyed the way their mirrored surfaces reflected the surrounding landscape, the sky, and other buildings. They also liked the fact that with reflective glass it didn't matter if the drapes in the windows were crooked or the blinds uneven; the building's facade still presented a uniform appearance. Others criticized reflective glass, however, saying that the reflections on its surface destroyed any sense of a separate, individual building.

Architects and homeowners used glass and windows in other ways to help overcome the effects of the energy crisis. They converted existing single-glazed windows into "twindow" units by installing second sheets of glass over the first. And they learned the importance of window management, making the best use of the sun's light and heat to save on fuel and electricity.

Many new homes built since the 1970s have been carefully positioned on their sites to take advantage of the sun. In winter the windows—particularly those facing south—act as passive solar collectors. They capture the sun's rays and reduce the need for mechanical heating as well as artificial lighting. In summer the householders cover the windows with awnings, shutters or sun screens to minimize heat and glare.

Even at the height of the energy crisis and urban unrest,

The Garden Grove Community Church in Garden Grove, California, designed by Philip Johnson and John Burgee and popularly known as "The Crystal Cathedral."

COURTESY OF JOHN BURGEE ARCHITECTS

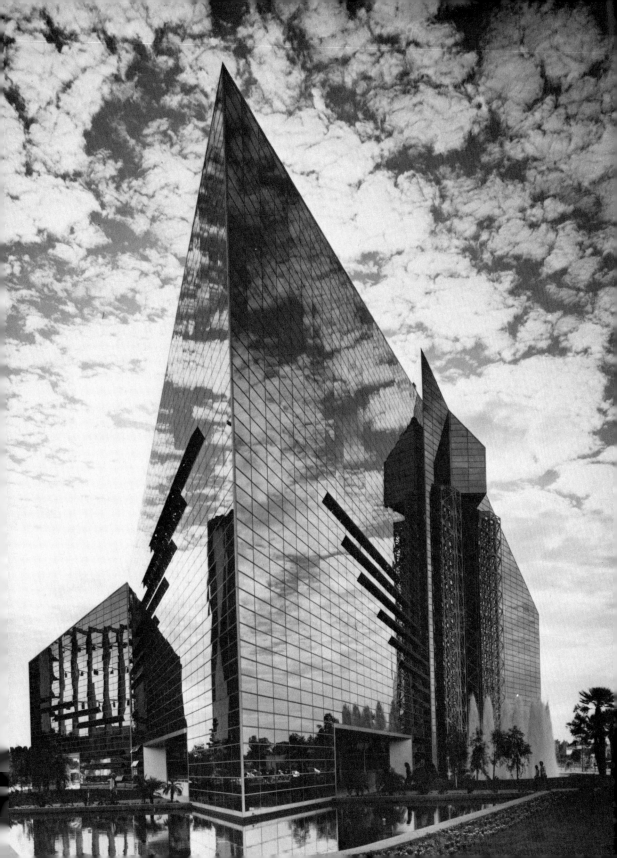

people never lost their desire for large window areas in their homes and places of work. In fact, studies showed that office and factory workers, and schoolchildren, were less cheerful and productive when they spent long hours in rooms without windows, lit only by artificial light. So it was only natural that as the crisis eased in the 1980s and the inner cities remained quiet, architects once more designed buildings with generous numbers of windows.

Inspired by advances in glass technology, the architects created churches, skyscrapers, and homes that treated windows in entirely new ways. Not surprisingly, Philip Johnson, the designer of the Glass House, collaborated on several of the most unusual glass buildings of the 1980s.

For the Reverend Robert H. Schuller, a television evangelist, Johnson and John Burgee built an all-glass church in Garden Grove, California. Shaped like a four-pointed star, the huge structure seats 3000 people and is covered entirely with reflective glass. This has earned it the nickname "The Crystal Cathedral." The glass screens out 92 percent of the sun's rays, creating a hushed underwater atmosphere within. During the service, the congregation sits surrounded by sky and changing weather, but nature seems transformed and softened by the reflective glass walls and roof.

Johnson and Burgee designed an even more striking group of glass buildings for PPG Industries in Pittsburgh, Pennsylvania. The complex serves as a symbol of its owner, best known as a manufacturer of architectural glass. It includes a forty-story tower, a thirteen-story tower, and four five-story buildings, arranged around a main plaza and sheathed in glass. Nearly 1,000,000 square feet of silver

The Gothic towers of PPG Place in Pittsburgh, designed by Philip Johnson and John Burgee.

insulating glass were needed to cover the six buildings.

Wanting the complex to be more than just another series of glass boxes, Johnson and Burgee turned to London's Houses of Parliament for inspiration and decorated the rooflines of the buildings with 231 Gothic-style glass spires. The walls of the towers and the other buildings are constructed of alternating square and triangular projections.

Everyone in the family enjoys the new sunspace.

From the inside they appear to be bay windows. On the outside they glitter with the passage of the sun and create fascinating reflections and rereflections.

In recent years all-glass structures have also become a common feature of many private homes. The sunroom, once better suited to plants than to people, has emerged as one of the most popular home-expansion ideas of the 1980s. Glass-roofed, glass-walled additions reach out from living and dining rooms, project from kitchens, and give master bedrooms a light, airy feel.

Sunrooms, or sunspaces, come in all sizes and shapes, from one-story leantos to two-story structures that wrap around a large portion of the house. Many sunrooms seem like direct descendants of Joseph Paxton's nineteenth-century conservatories, or smaller versions of Philip Johnson's Glass House.

The proud owner of a sunspace in Connecticut helped to explain their popularity when he said: "My wife and I are outdoor people, and we wanted to experience the various seasons. We've lit the exterior area with floodlights. That way we can be inside and eat dinner and see the snow coming down."

This couple, like their ancestors throughout history, enjoy watching what is going on outside while being protected from the elements. They reflect the same basic need for light and air that motivated early people to put openings in the walls of their dwellings; that inspired medieval church builders to create their miraculous windows of stained glass; and that led Ludwig Mies van der Rohe, Philip Johnson, and other twentieth-century architects to design skyscrapers and houses made entirely of glass.

The need for windows has survived wars, riots, and the collapse of great civilizations. It will no doubt continue to endure as long as people have eyes to see, hearts to feel, and a healthy curiosity about the world around them.

BIBLIOGRAPHY AND SOURCE NOTES
❖

This listing is organized by chapter, and in sequence within each chapter. As a result, it can be used to pursue a topic that the reader wants to explore further. Those books that were written for young people are indicated with asterisks. In addition to books and articles the listing includes mentions of exhibits, lectures, and tours that contributed importantly to the author's research.

Overall

Two histories of architecture were especially helpful to the author, and were referred to for almost all the chapters. Although lengthy and written for adults, they can be enjoyed by any reader with a strong interest in architecture. The books and their authors are:

Hamlin, Talbot. *Architecture Through the Ages.* New York: G. P. Putnam's Sons, 1940, 1953.

Jordan, R. Furneaux. *A Concise History of Western Architecture.* New York: Harcourt, Brace & World, Inc., 1970.

CHAPTER ONE

PREHISTORIC DWELLINGS AND WINDOWS

Giedion, Siegfried. *The Beginnings of Architecture: The Eternal Present, a Contribution on Constancy and Change.* Princeton, New Jersey: Princeton University Press, 1981

Rudofsky, Bernard. *The Prodigious Builders.* New York and London: Harcourt Brace Jovanovich, 1977; New York: Irvington Publishers, 1977

AFRICAN HOUSES

Andersen, Kaj Blegvad. *African Traditional Architecture.* Nairobi: Oxford University Press, 1977

ESKIMO DWELLINGS AND WINDOWS

Models and wall texts of a display that the author saw at the American Museum of Natural History, New York

ANCIENT RUSSIAN WINDOWS

Camesasca, Ettore, editor. *History of the House.* Translated by Isabel Quigly. New York: G. P. Putnam's Sons, 1971

MESOPOTAMIAN ARCHITECTURE

Hamlin, *Architecture Through the Ages*

CHAPTER TWO

CATAL HUYUK

Giedion. *The Beginnings of Architecture*

PUEBLO DWELLINGS AND WINDOWS

*Yue, Charlotte and David. *The Pueblo.* Boston: Houghton Mifflin Company, 1986

CANAANITE MYTH AND THE WORDS OF JEREMIAH
Rudofsky. *The Prodigious Builders*

WINDOWS IN ANCIENT EGYPTIAN HOMES AND TEMPLES
Hamlin. *Architecture Through the Ages*

Jordan. *A Concise History of Western Architecture*

CHAPTER THREE

CRETAN ARCHITECTURE
Hamlin. *Architecture Through the Ages*

WINDOWS IN GREEK HOUSES AND THE PARTHENON
Jordan. *A Concise History of Western Architecture*

ROMAN WINDOWS
*Andrews, Ian. *Pompeii.* London and New York: Cambridge University Press, 1978; Minneapolis: Lerner Publications, 1980

*Goor, Ron and Nancy. *Pompeii: Exploring a Roman Ghost Town.* New York: Thomas Y. Crowell, 1986

Hamlin. *Architecture Through the Ages*

Jordan. *A Concise History of Western Architecture*

McKay, Alexander G. *Houses, Villas, and Palaces in the Roman World.* Ithaca, N.Y.: Cornell University Press, 1975

Personal observations by the author of the Pantheon and other buildings in Rome

EARLY GLASSMAKING AND THE ANECDOTE FROM PLINY
Zerwick, Chloe. *A Short History of Glass.* Corning, N.Y.: Corning Museum of Glass, 1980

CHAPTER FOUR

CHINESE PAPERMAKING
Webb, Sheila. *Paper: The Continuous Thread.* Cleveland: The Cleveland Museum of Art, 1982

CHINESE HOMES AND WINDOWS
Gernet, Jacques. *Daily Life in China on the Eve of the Mongol Invasion, 1250–1276.* Stanford, California: Stanford University Press, 1970

The Editors of Horizon Magazine. *The Horizon Book of the Arts of China.* New York: American Heritage Publishing Co., Inc., 1969

Murck, Alfreda, and Wen Fong. *A Chinese Garden Court.* New York: The Metropolitan Museum of Art, 1980

JAPANESE HOMES AND WINDOWS
Itoh, Teiji. *Traditional Domestic Architecture of Japan.* Translated by Richard L. Gage. Tokyo: Heibonsha, 1965; New York: Weatherhill, 1972

Morse, Edward S. *Japanese Homes and Their Surroundings.* New York: Dover Publications, Inc., 1961

Nishihara, Kiyoyuki. *Japanese Houses: Patterns for Living.* Translated by Richard L. Gage. Tokyo and San Francisco: Japan Publications, Inc., 1967

CHAPTER FIVE

THE CHURCH OF ST. DENIS AND ITS WINDOWS
Duby, Georges and Robert Mandrou. *A History of French Civilization.* Translated by James Blakely Atkinson. New York: Random House, 1964

THE GOTHIC SYTLE OF ARCHITECTURE
Hamlin. *Architecture Through the Ages*
Jordan. *A Concise History of Western Architecture*

THE LAYOUT OF THE GREAT CATHEDRALS AND THE MEANING OF THEIR STAINED-GLASS WINDOWS

Temko, Allan. *Notre Dame de Paris.* New York: The Viking Press, Inc., 1955

THE MANUFACTURE OF STAINED-GLASS WINDOWS

Archer, Michael. *An Introduction to English Stained Glass.* London: Her Majesty's Stationery Office, 1985

Hayward, Jane. *Stained-Glass Windows.* New York: The Metropolitan Museum of Art Bulletin, December 1971–January 1972

Olmert, Michael. "Light for the Soul." Article in *Modern Maturity* magazine, December 1986–January 1987

*Watson, Percy. *Building the Medieval Cathedrals.* Cambridge: Cambridge University Press, 1976; Minneapolis: Lerner Publications, 1978

Zerwick. *A Short History of Glass*

Attendance by the author at a lecture on stained-glass windows and how they are made at the Cloisters branch of the Metropolitan Museum of Art in New York

THE ROSE WINDOWS OF NOTRE DAME AND THE WINDOWS OF SAINTE-CHAPELLE

Duby and Mandrou. *A History of French Civilization*

Temko. *Notre Dame de Paris*

Personal observations by the author on visits to Paris

CHAPTER SIX

CASTLE WINDOWS

*Giblin, James Cross. *Walls: Defenses Throughout History.* Boston: Little, Brown and Company, 1984

Gies, Joseph and Frances. *Life in a Medieval Castle.* New York: Harper & Row, Publishers, 1974

*Sancha, Sheila. *The Castle Story.* New York: Thomas Y. Crowell, 1979

WINDOWS IN MEDIEVAL VILLAGES AND TOWNS

Chambers, James. *The English House.* New York: W. W. Norton & Company, Inc., 1985

*Duke, Dulcie. *Lincoln: The Growth of a Medieval Town.* Cambridge: Cambridge University Press, 1974

Hamlin. *Architecture Through the Ages*

Holmes, Urban Tigner, Jr. *Daily Living in the Twelfth Century: Based on the Observations of Alexander Neckam in London and Paris.* Madison, Wisc.: The University of Wisconsin Press, 1952

Wood, Margaret. *The English Medieval House.* New York: Harper & Row Publishers, 1965

WINDOWS IN MOSLEM LANDS

Camesasca. *The History of the House*

CHAPTER SEVEN

STAINED-GLASS WINDOWS DURING THE PROTESTANT REFORMATION

Armitage, E. Liddall. *Stained Glass.* Newton, Mass.: Charles T. Branford Company, 1959

Brisac, Catherine. *A Thousand Years of Stained Glass.* New York: Doubleday and Co., Inc., 1986

FOREST GLASSHOUSES

Zerwick. *A Short History of Glass*

FRENCH RENAISSANCE CASTLES AND WINDOWS

Jordan. *A Concise History of Western Architecture*

ENGLISH COUNTRY HOUSES OF THE RENAISSANCE
> Chambers. *The English House*

DUTCH TOWN HOUSES OF THE SEVENTEENTH CENTURY
AND THEIR WINDOWS
> Rybczynski, Witold. *Home.* New York: Viking Penguin Inc., 1986

CHAPTER EIGHT

COLONIAL AMERICAN WINDOWS
> Hamlin. *Architecture Through the Ages*
>
> Kimball, Fiske. *Domestic Architecture of the American Colonies and of the Early Republic.* New York: Dover Publications, Inc., 1966
>
> Wall texts and captions from an exhibit on life in colonial America between 1620 and 1776, observed by the author at the National Museum of American History in Washington, D.C.

GLASSMAKING IN COLONIAL AMERICA
> Zerwick. *A Short History of Glass*

THE AMERICAN LOG CABIN
> Bealer, Alex W. and John O. Ellis. *The Log Cabin.* Barre, Mass.: Barre Publishing, 1978

ENGLISH MASS PRODUCTION OF PLATE GLASS
> *Cunningham, Colin. *Building for the Victorians.* Cambridge: Cambridge University Press, 1985

JOSEPH PAXTON AND HIS CONSERVATORIES
> Hix, John. *The Glass House.* Cambridge, Mass.: The MIT Press, 1974

THE LONDON CRYSTAL PALACE

*Cunningham. *Building for the Victorians*

Hix. *The Glass House*

Wall texts and captions from an exhibit on Crystal Palaces, observed by the author at the Cooper-Hewitt Museum in New York

THE NEW YORK CRYSTAL PALACE

Gayle, Margot, and Stephen Garmey. *The New York Crystal Palace, 1853/58* (pamphlet). New York: Friends of Cast-Iron Architecture, 1974

Hix. *The Glass House*

Wall texts and captions from the Cooper-Hewitt exhibit

CAST-IRON BUILDING FRONTS

Gayle, Margot, and Edmund V. Gillon, Jr. *Cast-Iron Architecture in New York*. New York: Dover Publications, Inc., 1974

CHAPTER NINE

NINETEENTH-CENTURY STAINED-GLASS WINDOWS

Burke, Doreen Bolger, and others. *In Pursuit of Beauty: Americans and the Aesthetic Movement*. New York: The Metropolitan Museum of Art, 1986

Wilson, H. Weber. *Great Glass in American Architecture*. New York: E. P. Dutton, 1986

Personal observations by the author at Calvary Church, New York, and at the Metropolitan Museum of Art in the same city

JOHN LA FARGE

Adams, Henry. "John La Farge, the Inventive Maverick." Article in *Smithsonian* magazine, July, 1987

Burke and others. *In Pursuit of Beauty*

LOUIS COMFORT TIFFANY

Burke and others. *In Pursuit of Beauty*

Cohen, Daniel. "Splendor in Glass." Article in *Historic Preservation*, July/August 1987

Koch, Robert. *Louis C. Tiffany: Rebel in Glass.* New York: Crown Publishers, Inc., 1964

Wilson. *Great Glass in American Architecture*

FRANK LLOYD WRIGHT

Hamlin. *Architecture Through the Ages*

Hanks, David A. *The Decorative Designs of Frank Lloyd Wright.* New York: E. P. Dutton, 1979

Jordan. *A Concise History of Western Architecture*

Kaufmann, Edgar, Jr. *Frank Lloyd Wright at the Metropolitan Museum of Art.* New York: The Metropolitan Museum of Art, 1982

Lipman, Jonathan. *Frank Lloyd Wright and the Johnson Wax Buildings.* New York: Rizzoli International Publications, Inc., 1986

Personal observations by the author at the Metropolitan Museum of Art and the Museum of Modern Art, both in New York

CHAPTER TEN

EARLY CHICAGO SKYSCRAPERS

*Giblin, James Cross. *The Skyscraper Book.* New York: Thomas Y. Crowell, 1981

THE RELIANCE BUILDING

Condit, Carl W. *The Chicago School of Architecture.* Chicago and London: The University of Chicago Press, 1964

Legner, Linda. *Reliance Building* (brochure). Chicago: Commission on Chicago Historical and Architectural Landmarks, 1979

Personal observations by the author

DISPLAY WINDOWS

Marcus, Leonard S. *The American Store Window.* New York: Whitney Library of Design, Watson-Guptill Publications, 1978

FAGUS FACTORY

Jordan. *A Concise History of Western Architecture*

PAUL SCHEERBART'S THOUGHTS ON GLASS-WALLED BUILDINGS

Hix. *The Glass House*

THE HALLIDIE BUILDING

Corbett, Michael R. *Splendid Survivors.* San Francisco: A California Living Book, 1979

Newspaper descriptions of the building at the time it opened, from the files of the Foundation for San Francisco's Architectural Heritage

Personal observations by the author

MIES VAN DER ROHE'S 1920s SKYSCRAPER PROJECTS

Eckhardt, Wolf van. *A Place to Live: The Crisis of the Cities.* New York: The Delacorte Press (A Seymour Lawrence Book), 1967

Johnson, Philip. *Mies van der Rohe.* New York: The Museum of Modern Art, 1978

PHILADELPHIA SAVINGS FUND SOCIETY BUILDING AND SCHOCKEN DEPARTMENT STORE

Jordy, William H. *American Buildings and Their Architects: The Impact of European Modernism in the Mid-Twentieth Century.* Garden City, N.Y.: Anchor Press/Doubleday, 1976

KRISTALLNACHT

Davidowicz, Lucy S. *The War Against the Jews: 1933–1945.* New York: Holt, Rinehart and Winston, 1975

Wigoder, Geoffrey. *The Story of the Synagogue.* San Francisco: Harper & Row, Publishers, 1986

THE BLITZ (AND ANECDOTE ABOUT NEVILLE CHAMBER-LAIN)

Thompson, Laurence. *1940.* New York: William Morrow and Company, Inc., 1966

DRESDEN BOMBING

Guide, German Democratic Republic. Dresden: Verlag Zeit im Bild, 1972

RAIDS ON HIROSHIMA AND NAGASAKI

Committee for the Compilation of Materials on Damage Caused by the Atomic Bombs in Hiroshima and Nagasaki. *Hiroshima and Nagasaki: The Physical, Medical, and Social Effects of the Atomic Bombings.* New York: Basic Books, Inc., 1981

CHAPTER ELEVEN

LEVER HOUSE

Descriptive brochure produced by Lever Brothers Company

MIES' LAKE SHORE DRIVE APARTMENTS IN CHICAGO AND SEAGRAM BUILDING IN NEW YORK

Jordy. *American Buildings and Their Architects*
Pomaranc, Joan C. *860–880 Lake Shore Drive* (brochure). Chicago: Commission on Chicago Historical and Architectural Landmarks, 1980

POSTWAR SUBURBAN HOUSES

The Romance of Glass (brochure). Pittsburgh: PPG Industries, 1982

PHILIP JOHNSON'S GLASS HOUSE

Knight, Carleton III. "Philip Johnson Sounds Off." Interview in *Historic Preservation*, September/October, 1986

Philip Johnson in New Canaan. New Canaan, Connecticut: The New Canaan Historical Society Annual, 1986

Tributes to Mr. Johnson that appeared in *The New York Times* and *The Los Angeles Times* on the occasion of his 80th birthday in July 1986

Information supplied to the author by John Burgee Architects

CHAPTER TWELVE

EFFECTS OF POLLUTION ON STAINED-GLASS WINDOWS

Frenzel, Gottfried. "The Restoration of Medieval Stained Glass." Article in *Scientific American*, February, 1987

POSTWAR VANDALISM

*Madison, Arnold. *Vandalism: The Not-So-Senseless Crime*. New York: Clarion Books, 1970

RIOTS IN THE 1960s

*Heaps, Willard A. *Riots, U.S.A.: 1765–1970*, revised edition. New York: Clarion Books, 1970

REFLECTIVE GLASS IN WINDOWS

The Romance of Glass (PPG Industries)

THE CRYSTAL CATHEDRAL AND PPG PLACE

Information supplied to the author by John Burgee Architects and PPG Industries

MODERN SUNROOMS

Langdon, Philip. "Greenhouses Bloom into Sunspaces." Article in *The New York Times*, February 5, 1987

INDEX

❖

Page numbers in italic type refer to illustrations.

EDUCATION